Sasha

Sasha

A very special 'Dog Tale'
of a very special 'Epi-Dog'

Brian L Porter

To Sasha

Who fills so many hearts
with sunshine and joy

And for epileptic dogs everywhere

With special thanks to the veterinary surgeons, nurses and
administrative staff at the Doncaster, Yorkshire branch of Vets 4 Pets
who have proved to be Sasha's lifeline in her darkest times.

A Short Glossary

Mostly for our American friends, a short explanation of a couple of language differences.

Epi-dog = a term used by many epileptic dog owners to classify their dogs.
Lead = leash
Dry food = kibble
Staffy = Staffordshire Bull Terrier

Introduction

Sasha is, at the time of writing, a five year old Staffordshire Bull Terrier, who is quite simply one of the most amazing animals it has been my privilege to know in my lifetime. Abandoned in a gutter at just six weeks old, she was almost dead from hypothermia when she was found by a passing dog warden. One week later she became a part of our family and what follows in this book is quite simply the story of a brave, resilient, and most importantly exuberantly happy dog, who despite the many and varied trials and tribulations that life has thrown her way, remains, in my estimation, 'the happiest dog on the planet.'

Acknowledgements

Where do I begin to thank all the people who have been of help, not just in creating this book, but in helping Sasha live the most normal life she can, despite the multiple setbacks she's suffered in her life?

First and foremost, my undying thanks go to Rebecca, Bernard, Ben, John and all the other vets who have helped Sasha over the years, through her original hypothermia, subsequent broken legs, skin allergies, and multiple epileptic seizures. At one point, not long ago, after a series of non-stop seizures which you'll read about in this book, we honestly thought we were losing our brave little dog. Thanks to the dedication, care and love given to her by all the vets, nurses and staff members at our veterinary surgery including Lynne, Suzanne, Sarah, Isobel, Diane, Karina, Claire, Lisa, Sam, Kirsty, Sharon, Charlotte, Camilla, Helen, Becky, Carl and anyone whose names I may have missed out, she survived and was returned to us against all odds.

I'm also grateful to the staff at the emergency veterinarian hospital who provided her with in-patient care most recently after her multiple seizures and of course, to the specialists who treated her and rebuilt her leg joint not just once, but twice in her early months of life. Without their dedication and expertise we wouldn't have the pleasure and the joy of sharing Sasha's life as we do.

Thanks also to my fellow author and dear friend Ed Cook who surprised me one day by announcing he had started a Facebook page for Sasha. 'Sasha the Wagging Tail of England' gathered over one hundred followers in its first twenty four hours and her followers continue to grow.

One of Sasha's most ardent followers is her 'Aunty Carole' otherwise known as bestselling horror author Carole Gill. Carole has always followed Sasha's life and long ago fell under her spell and loves her dearly, so much so that she recently named her new kitten, 'Sasha' what else? Carole has been so supportive through some of the worst moments in Sasha's life, always there to offer words of comfort and helpful advice when I've been so worried about my 'baby girl.'

Thanks go to Miika Hannila at Creativia Publishing, who is not only my publisher but yet another dog lover and an ardent follower of the life of Sasha. Thank you for publishing her story, Miika.

My novels are usually subjected to the skilful Beta reading of Debbie Poole, who agreed to give this manuscript her attention when I told her about it. Not only that, but her creative skills were so vital in helping me to produce the final cover design for the book. Thanks again Debbie, for everything.

My cousin, Barbara Francis spent many hours on her knees in church, despite her age and infirmity praying for Sasha and lit candles for her and added her to the church's 'sick list' for additional prayers. Thank you so much my wonderfully loving and caring cousin and also everyone else who prayed for Sasha in her darkest moments, including Lorna Donaldson in Scotland who cares so deeply for Sasha, and Jakki Barlow who lost her own dear Ramsay to the same illness and who now follows Sasha's life closely.

My wife, Juliet of course shares in the daily task of caring for Sasha and all our other dogs, as groomer, carer, and dog walker. She also shares in the worry and the fear that go hand-in-hand with life with Sasha. Thank you Juliet, we couldn't manage without you.

There are so many people who have helped along the way that I know I must have left some out of this list of acknowledgements. If I have, please accept my apologies and know that I appreciate every bit of help that has been offered both in creating this book and in helping Sasha to live a normal life. I thank you all and can only hope she goes on to enjoy many more years of happiness and keeps that tail wagging more and more every day. Perhaps we'll see you on her Facebook page one day. You'll be very welcome.

See Sasha's Facebook page at
https://www.facebook.com/groups/270003923193039/

Contents

1   Puppy Power!   1

2   'Baby Girl'   4

3   Disaster Looms   8

4   Accident!   11

5   Post-operative Care   21

6   Déjà Vu   26

7   Good Times, Bad Times   37

8   Best Friend, Sheba   41

9   The Puppies   48

10   Fit   51

11   Research & Reactions   57

12   More friends   66

13   Emergency!   73

14   The Third Day   84

15   Homecoming   88

16   A New Problem for Sasha   95

Chapter 1

Puppy Power!

Christmas had come and gone, and winter was proving a difficult adversary for anyone looking forward to a break in the icy cold weather we were facing. My wife and I, together with our two girls, decided, one cold, bleak January morning to pay a visit to our local dog pound. Let me explain here that my wife and I are what might be described as 'dedicated' dog rescuers. Our home was, and still is, home to a number of wonderful dogs, all of whom have been subjected to abuse or neglect in their previous lives. We have adopted each one with a view to providing them with the care, love, affection and security and every one of them is an important member of our family.

From the worst case of abuse, Sheba, once used as bait to train fighting dogs, to Dexter, thrown from a moving car at high speed on a busy motorway, Dylan, beaten within an inch of his life as a puppy, or Penny, abandoned on a railway line when her 'family' of travellers moved on, these and all our dogs have responded to our care by rewarding us with the unconditional love that only a dog seems capable of giving to its owner.

So, returning to our visit to the dog pound, we'd adopted a number of dogs from there in the past and knowing and appreciating the hard work that the staff there put in to their care for the often pathetic and unwanted dogs that found their way to the pound, we arrived with a gift of a large box of chocolates for the girls who cared for the dogs on a daily basis. While there, one of the girls took us into the rear office where, in a small dog crate, we saw a tiny, white puppy, with black markings, a Staffordshire Bull Terrier no bigger than a small rabbit. As soon as she saw us, the puppy went straight into 'take me home' mode, her tiny tail wagging at about a hundred miles per hour and her little tongue hanging out in anticipation of some treat or affection. We were instantly smitten, even more so when the lady at the pound took the puppy out of the crate and placed her in my wife's arms. After a minute, Juliet passed the pup to me, and it was clear to see; we had to have this little bundle, so small she was able to comfortably fit in the palm of my hand.

The whole decision-making process had taken no more than two minutes and we began filling out the paperwork that would allow us to adopt the puppy, who we placed on the floor and watched as we filled in the forms. The tiny pup dashed here and there, ran in circles, then back and forth over the length of the office floor, her tail never still as it wagged with happiness.

Paperwork complete, we now faced an agonising wait as the rules relating to stray dogs meant the dog had to be held in the pound for seven days, just in case the original owner turned up to claim their missing dog.

The chances of that happening in this case, were, we were assured virtually zero as the puppy had been found in the gutter on a lonely street, shivering and almost dead from hypothermia, by a passing dog warden who did in fact think it was a dead rabbit lying in the gutter as she drove along the street. Thankfully she pulled up to investigate and found the tiny puppy, barely alive and took her straight to the pound where she was gradually warmed up, examined by their vet, fed and watered and soon seemed none the worse for her ordeal. The warden estimated the pup as being no more than six weeks old and certainly too young to have left her mother. The staff at the pound explained they were feeding her on puppy milk bought from a local pet food specialist as she was too young to have been fully weaned on to solid food.

Confident that the puppy would soon be joining our family we drove home and spent the next few days preparing for our new arrival. We visited the pet store and bought her a nice soft, warm dog bed, with a lovely fleecy blanket to go in it to make sure she was warm in her bed. Dog toys came next, together with an adequate supply of puppy milk and a bowl for her food. It would be a while before she could go for walks in public, as she would have to have her inoculations beforehand, but we did invest in a collar and lead for her, ready for the first time she went out for a walk in the big, wide world. Having measured her neck at the pound we found she was far too small for even the smallest dog collar available, so we eventually purchased a small cat collar with a little bell attached. At least our new puppy wouldn't get easily lost once she came home. The bell would make sure of that.

Perhaps the most important decision we made in the days leading up to her coming home for the first time was in deciding on her name. After numerous suggestions were put forth by my wife, me and the girls, we finally reached a decision and the next day I ordered a new shiny name tag for our puppy. Henceforth she was no longer 'the puppy.'

Her name was Sasha!

Chapter 2

'Baby Girl'

Finally, the waiting period was over and we motored across town to collect our new 'baby girl' from the dog pound. Full of excitement, we parked the car in their car park and walked into the office where we were met by smiles from the two girls on duty that day. One of them went to fetch Sasha as the other young lady filled out the remaining necessary paperwork and took my adoption fee and gave me the receipt which meant that Sasha was now legally ours.

Louise came back into the office with little Sasha in her arms and handed her to Juliet. Sasha's tail just never stopped wagging, much as she'd behaved the first time we saw her. Little did we know that cold January day that Sasha's wagging tail would prove to be her 'trademark' over the coming years and would even inspire an American friend of mine to create a webpage for her on Facebook, but more of that later.

For now, we were delighted to have our new puppy and Juliet sat in the car's passenger seat, cuddling Sasha, wrapped in a fleecy blanket as I drove home.

If we'd harboured any fears or worries about how our other dogs might react when we arrived home with this new tiny interloper on their territory, they were dispelled within minutes of Sasha being introduced to them. We let her roam around in the garden and allowed the other dogs to come and see her a couple at a time. It was obvious she was a hit with the other members of our 'pack' as the only reaction we got from them was that they all seemed to want to play with her. That tail of hers wagged and wagged as she went from one dog to another, indulging in what we saw as 'doggie introductions.' She looked so small and frail next to our other dogs, but she held no fear of them and immediately made herself at home. We allowed them all to get to know each other before eventually allowing Sasha into the house for the first time.

The next hour or so was hilarious as she went everywhere, exploring her new home and surroundings. Like Goldilocks, she tottered around the kitchen, trying out each and every bed, sniffing at the two large water bowls we always keep filled for the dogs, and as we allowed her to progress from room to room her inquisitiveness saw her sticking her head into every nook and cranny, under chairs, tables, behind the TV, and taking great interest in every new sight, everything being new to her, the start of life's great adventure for little Sasha. Already, it appeared as if our eldest Staffordshire Bull Terrier, (henceforth referred to in this book as 'Staffies'), Sheba, was showing great interest in Sasha, following her around like a canine chaperone, and it has been no surprise over the years that the two of them have become firm and fast 'best friends'. I'll tell you more about the breed make-up of our pack a little later,

It wasn't long before tiredness began to catch up with our baby girl, a term of endearment that has stayed with her to this day. If we're talking to Sasha it is quite normal for us to refer to her as 'Baby Girl' and she responds to that name in the same way she does to her true name.

My wife picked her up and placed her gently in the cosy new bed we'd bought especially for her. As well as a nice fleecy padded cushion, the bed contained a couple of dog toys we'd bought in readiness for her arrival. Almost as if she knew it was hers, Sasha sniffed at the toys, then promptly ignored them and fell fast asleep. The other dogs must have sensed she was young and vulnerable because, until she woke naturally after sleeping for almost an hour, not one of them disturbed her. One or two walked up to her bed, sniffing at the tiny bundle lying there, her eyes tightly closed, but not one dog did anything that might have woken her. Even then on that first day, we should have realised there was something special about Sasha.

Feeding time soon came round as Sasha woke up and being so young, we knew she needed feeding little but often. Having purchased a supply of puppy milk from our pet store prior to her arrival we were ready and waiting to feed our hungry puppy. Sure enough, she lapped it up and was then ready for playtime, which involved me, my wife, Sasha and most of the other dogs. They all loved running around and playing with the new addition to the family, though a couple of them were a little suspicious of the fact that the new puppy gave off a ringing sound as she ran. The bell on the cat collar had much to answer for. Being so young, she quickly grew tired and much to our surprise, she went directly to her own bed, flopped onto her cushion and was asleep in seconds.

Later still, when it was time to feed the rest of our dogs, despite her tender age and the fact she wasn't really ready for solid food, Sasha decided she wanted to know what the others had all got and so inquisitively ran up to where Sheba was eating and began sniffing at her bowl. Rather than snapping or growling at her as we might have expected, Sheba allowed the tiny pup to sniff at her food, and then tentatively, Sasha took a tiny mouthful and wow, she simply devoured it. From that day we made sure she received a small portion of 'grown up' dog food each day to supplement her puppy milk and so began the process of weaning her, right from day one.

As is normal with the arrival of any new dog in a household, the first day seemed to fly by, and before we knew it, bedtime had arrived. Being so small, we'd decided to have Sasha in our bedroom and so carried her bed up the stairs to our bedroom where we placed it beside the bed near to Juliet. At that time we had another dog, Dinky, who was relatively new and who also slept in our room. Before we knew it, Sasha had curled up with Dinky and the two little dogs were soon fast asleep. I fully expected to have to get up in the night to let Sasha out to do her business, or take a pee, but the puppy slept right through the night and held on until we rose in the morning and let her out in the garden. The other thing we found that first morning was that between them, Sasha and Dinky had somehow pulled the big blue blanket from Dinky's bed out onto the floor where the pair of them had made a kind of 'nest' and were happily snoring together as we awoke.

The first day and night had come and gone and passed like a dream. Sasha had made a real impression on all of us, human and canine!

Chapter 3

Disaster Looms

The first couple of weeks of Sasha's life in our home went as expected, with much fun, laughter and excitement at watching our new puppy integrate herself into life with the other dogs as well as with us. From day one, this beautiful little foundling impressed us with the fact she didn't have one single toilet 'accident' in the home, dutifully toddling after any of the other dogs who went out into the garden and doing whatever she had to do in the area where our dogs had been trained to 'do their business.' We were astounded at this fact, as in all the years my wife and I had been keeping dogs, we'd never yet come across one that required no specific training in toilet matters.

She knew from day one which bed was hers and unlike the other dogs who kind of 'shared' the beds in the kitchen during the day, Sasha would unerringly home in on her own bed when she wanted to rest or sleep, and curl up contentedly.

A visit to the vet for a health check and her first round of vaccinations not only went well, it marked the beginning of a life-long love affair between the staff and vets at the practice and Sasha, a dog who even at her tender age had found a way into the hearts of everyone she came into contact with.

Very early in life, Sasha developed a love of what would become and still is her favourite dog treat, so we always have a supply of 'gravy bones" handy.

Around this time, Juliet and I were seriously considering the possibility of owning our own kennels, a long-held ambition for both of us. It was our dream to run such an establishment and at the same time, Juliet could use her dog grooming experience to offer a grooming facility and our friend, a qualified canine behaviourist was keen to rent space from us where he could offer dog training sessions in a secure and protected environment. We also hoped to have a small on-site shop where we would sell dog food, accessories and anything dog-related. We saw a suitable business advertised for sale a few miles from our home and made arrangements to go along to view it. Not wanting to leave Sasha at home while we visited the property, we loaded her into the back of the car along with a couple of our other dogs for company and enjoyed a great visit to the kennels, where the owners fell head-over-heels in love with our gorgeous and exuberant puppy, whose antics and personality succeeded in captivating them from the minute we took her out of the car and allowed her to run around in their exercise area.

Before we left that day, having arranged to go back for a second visit later in the week to examine the kennel's financial records, there were lots of jokes being thrown around about the kennel owners 'kidnapping' Sasha, so greatly had they fallen for her. The little puppy simply loved riding in the car, even though she was so small she couldn't actually see much out of the window, even standing on her hind legs, but she tried, she really tried.

When we arrived for the second visit a few days later, the owners seemed more delighted to see Sasha than us, and I'm sure we would have got round to viewing the books much sooner if it hadn't been for the constant attention she was subjected to. Eventually we took our leave once again and it would be some weeks before we finally decided not to proceed with the purchase of the kennels. Sasha enjoyed her tea that evening and as usual slept the sleep of the innocent later that night, curled up on the blue blanket together with Dinky. It would prove to be the last good night's sleep she, or any of us would enjoy for quite some time.

Chapter 4

Accident!

The morning after the visit to the kennels saw everything begin as normal. There was no hint of the tragedy to come as the girls got ready for school and Juliet and I did our usual early morning dog walks with the other dogs.

Sasha was her usual self, bouncing around with joy and happiness, playing with Dinky as she always did first thing in the morning. With the girls gone and Juliet walking four dogs, I was upstairs, getting washed in the bathroom, leaving the door open so I could keep an eye on the puppy as she played.

The thing none of us had considered was that the upstairs landing which ran from the bathroom to each of our three bedrooms, and joined the stairs in a junction close to the bathroom, though railed off from the stairs side, contained a small gap, no more than four inches high, between the landing and the descending stairs.

As I was getting ready, I checked every ten seconds or so to see that all was well and that Dinky wasn't becoming too rough in her play with Sasha. Suddenly, I heard a squeal, a loud one, and when I turned to look, I saw no sign of the puppy.

Running from the bedroom, I looked but couldn't see Sasha anywhere. I heard another squeal, this time more of a whimper and realised it was coming from downstairs. How could it be possible?

I'd fitted a baby gate at the top of the stairs to prevent her accidentally falling downstairs, but to my eternal regret, neither I nor Juliet had thought that the tiny gap on the landing would prove to be so calamitous.

Sasha had clearly been playing with Dinky and had managed to somehow fall through that tiny gap and had landed at least twelve feet below in the hallway. I reacted instantly and ran downstairs to check on my baby girl. Poor little Sasha was lying on her side with her right leg sticking out at an impossible angle!

I stroked and loved her, feeling wretched and blaming myself for what had taken place, but this was no time for such thoughts. I gently picked her up, and her little tail as usual started wagging despite what must have been the terrible pain she must have felt. Thankfully, Juliet arrived home a couple of minutes later and together, we examined her closely. We both realised her injury was serious and I phoned the vet and was instructed to take Sasha there as soon as possible.

Within minutes, I was on my way. Due to her injury, there was no way she could be placed in the back of the car unattended and Juliet quickly found an old ladies wicker shopping basket, one of those with the handle that goes over the top from side to side, and lined it with a blanket. She placed Sasha so gently into the basket and put both dog and basket on the passenger seat of the car. Though she wanted to come with me, I told her to stay and look after the other dogs, not wanting her to be there if the vet gave me really bad news. The possibility existed in my mind that they might not be able to operate on a puppy so young and that we might lose little Sasha before she'd had a chance to enjoy life at all.

A quick but thorough examination by Rebecca, who has been Sasha's vet since day one, confirmed our fears that she'd suffered a fracture to her elbow joint. For those unfamiliar with canine anatomy, that's the joint at the top of the leg where it joins the shoulder. They would have to x-ray the joint to assess the extent of the damage and I had to leave Sasha at the vet's while they carried out the procedure, having given her a painkilling injection before I left her in their care.

Arriving home, both Juliet and I found ourselves barely able to function as we worried and fretted about what was happening to our baby girl, our gorgeous Sasha! We were grateful the girls had been at school when Sasha's accident occurred. At least they'd been spared having to go to school feeling upset and filled with the fears and worries we were sharing at that time. Juliet refused to blame me for the accident, and in truth, that's what it was, an awful, tragic accident that nobody could have foreseen. We simply hadn't taken into account just how tiny Sasha was and the thought that she might actually fit through that miniscule gap at the top of the stairs hadn't entered either of our minds for a second. To fill in some of the waiting time, I went to the local shops and bought a piece of hardboard which I painted with quick-drying woodstain and fitted it to the existing rails along the length of the landing. It may have been a case of shutting the stable door after the horse had bolted, but at least I'd made sure such an accident could never happen again in the future. We could only hope during those terrible hours of waiting that Sasha would actually have a future. Thoughts of the cost of any treatment Sasha may need came to mind and we were grateful that when we'd adopted her from the pound we'd been issued with a certificate granting her six weeks free pet insurance, so at least we could feel secure in the knowledge that her injury would be covered by the insurance. We always insure our dogs anyway, and it was obvious we'd have to stay with the same insurer when the free period expired as no other company would henceforth cover her for previous injuries such as this and it was very clear that her treatment would be ongoing and go on long beyond the six weeks free period. Unfortunately, though the company providing the free insurance was a large and reputable pet insurance company, it was also known for being expensive by comparison with other similar companies, but we knew we had no choice, and Sasha would have to stay covered by the company concerned for the remainder of her life, a small price to pay, we decided. I mention this here because as time went on we grew more and more grateful for that insurance and can honestly say that all pet owners should ensure their dog, cat, rabbit or whatever pet it may be is insured, as we have learned over the years the value of having our pets and Sasha in particular, covered by the best insurance we can afford.

* * *

A very long four hours slowly ticked by. Juliet and I continued to worry, wanting to pick up the phone and ask how she was doing, but we knew they would call as soon as they had something to tell us. Eventually, the phone rang. My hand actually trembled as I picked it up, the caller I.D. function informing me it was the vet calling. What would they say?

I answered with great trepidation, saying a small prayer as I did so. "Mr. Porter?"

"Hello Rebecca," I replied, nervously. "How is she?"

"Sasha's x-rays show that she has sustained a fracture to her elbow joint as I thought this morning. We can repair it, but she'll need to be transferred to a specialist veterinarian hospital in Manchester where we have the services of a consultant orthopaedic surgeon on hand. He can operate on her tomorrow, and Sasha will need to have the joint pinned and have a plate inserted to hold the joint in place, which will be screwed in place and will then require a long period of rest and recuperation."

Although this wasn't exactly good news, it was far better than the worst case scenario Juliet and I had been terrifying ourselves with.

"Okay, thanks, Rebecca," I replied. "What happens now?"

"Can you come in to the practice now and fill in the necessary forms which will give us permission to go ahead with the operation?"

"I'll be there within half an hour, Rebecca," I said, and hung up and quickly explained everything to Juliet before jumping into the car and driving to the vet's surgery as fast as the speed limits allowed.

On arriving at the surgery I was taken through to the treatment area where little Sasha was in one of the large cages used for in-patients. She looked so tiny and pathetic, and yet as soon as she saw me she began wagging that amazing little tail of hers. Rebecca came to me and quickly ran through everything she'd told me on the phone for a second time, just to be sure I was fully aware of what needed to be done. I signed the necessary documents that would allow them to carry out the operation on her broken leg and Rebecca explained that Sasha would be taken the fifty miles to Manchester by pet ambulance and would spend the night at the pet hospital there before the surgeon would carry out her operation the next morning. If all went well, they would wait until she'd recovered from the operation and the effects of the anaesthetic had worn off before transporting her back to the surgery, after which I could collect her and take her home.

Amazed and impressed at how fast they were going ahead with everything, I asked if I could spend a few minutes with Sasha before leaving her in their care again.

"Spend as long as you like," Rebecca replied, kindly. "She's such a beautiful little puppy, and so happy despite her pain."

Even at this early juncture in her life, Sasha was making her way inexorably into the hearts of the staff at the veterinary practice, a place she's held ever since, even with the changes to personnel that inevitably occur over the years in such businesses.

Leaving Sasha there soon afterwards was a heartbreaking necessity. I knew she was in good hands and would be well cared for, but, even in her sleepy state as a result of the sedatives she'd been given before her x-rays, she seemed to know I was going away and her eyes virtually pleaded with me to take her with me, her tail wagging as always, though not quite as fast as was usual. I stroked her, bent into the cage and kissed the top of her tiny head, and said a quiet "bye for now, I'll see you tomorrow" to her and then turned away with a tear in my eye.

"She'll be fine, Mr. Porter," Rebecca the vet said to me as I stood a little forlornly at the door to the vet's surgery, not really wanting to go home and yet knowing I was doing no good by just waiting there, achieving nothing.

Clinging to those words from Sasha's vet, I drove home very slowly with tears pricking at my eyes as I did so. Not normally given to such emotional displays, I still felt responsible for the accident and knew I wouldn't feel myself again until I knew the following day's operation had been successfully completed and Sasha was home with us once again, where she belonged.

By the time I arrived home, the girls had returned from school and as usual, looked for the puppy. Juliet told them what had happened and their fears and worries were now added to those of me and my wife. That evening was one of the longest I can remember and the night even more so, as sleep evaded me, Juliet too, as we both continued to think about Sasha and the ordeal that awaited her the next day.

The morning of Sasha's operation dawned, with Juliet and I looking and feeling drawn, exhausted and filled with trepidation for what lay ahead that day. There are always risks attached whenever a dog has to be given anaesthetics prior to an operation, hence the consent form the owner has to sign to give the veterinary surgeon permission to carry out the procedure. With Sasha being so young and knowing the weakened state she'd been in just a few short weeks previously, our fears were naturally heightened.

"When will Sasha be coming home?" Victoria, at 11 years old, our youngest girl asked as soon as she came downstairs for breakfast.

"We won't know until the vet calls us later," Juliet told her.

"They're operating as early as possible this morning," I added, "to give her as much time to recover afterwards before they bring her back to our vet's surgery sometime this afternoon. Once Rebecca has checked that everything is okay, she'll let me know when I can go and pick Sasha up."

"She's going to be okay, isn't she?" Victoria asked me.

"I hope so, Victoria, I really hope so," I replied. What more could I say? I tried to be as honest as possible with Victoria, without worrying her unduly. There was no need at that stage to place any more fears or worries in her young mind. Rebecca, the eldest who shared her name with Sasha's vet, said very little, keeping her fears for our puppy very much to herself.

Both girls went to school that morning as usual but I'm sure neither of their minds was on their lessons throughout that day. Like mine and Juliet's they were focussed solely on events outside our control, taking place over fifty miles away.

The day wore on relentlessly, each hour passing interminably slowly, as Juliet and I waited for news. We walked the other dogs in shifts between us, a couple at a time. Juliet drank tea, I drank coffee, lots of it. We stared at the phone, willing it to ring. We walked from room to room in an aimless quest to try to make the time pass quicker, with no discernible success.

Even the other dogs sensed something was wrong. Sheba and Dinky in particular were extremely restless, each of them periodically walking up to Sasha's little bed, sniffing it as though looking for her. They couldn't work out where there new little friend was.

I'm sure we've all had certain moments in our lives where we've been so agitated and so hyped up with emotion that physical symptoms begin to manifest themselves. That was certainly the case that day as both Juliet and I began to suffer intense headaches and had to take tablets to counter their effects.

Two o'clock came and went; then three o'clock and still no word. How many times did I contemplate picking up the phone just to call the vet and ask for news, but I stopped myself, knowing that even if Sasha had been returned to them, she would in all probability still be under the effects of anaesthetic or being monitored to ensure all was well, so any calls from me would merely serve as unnecessary interruptions.

Four o'clock had just registered on the clock when the phone began ringing. Juliet and I engaged in a race to pick it up and Juliet, not hindered by physical disability as I am, was the obvious winner. When she looked at the phone however and saw the vet's number on the caller I.D. screen, she 'chickened out' and passed the phone to me.

"It's them," she gasped. "I can't talk to them, here, you do it."

Sure enough, it was Rebecca.

"How is she, Rebecca?" I blurted out, breathlessly.

"Sasha's fine, Mr. Porter."

I gave Juliet a thumbs-up sign to say all was well as I listened to the rest of Rebecca's news.

"The operation went well, and she's been back here with us for about an hour and a half. She's still a bit dopey, but if you want to come in, in about half an hour, I can go through everything with you and then you'll be able to take Sasha home."

I really can't remember what I said after that but after completing my conversation with Rebecca, I told Juliet what she'd said and we hugged each other as a sense of relief flooded through us both.

The girls arrived home from school as I was leaving in the car to go and collect Sasha and were excited and relieved and couldn't wait for me to return with what would still be our still very poorly puppy.

* * *

Sasha looked so vulnerable when Rebecca carried her in to the treatment room soon after my arrival at the surgery. Her right leg was fully encased in a veterinarian bandage and another smaller bandage was in place on her left leg where they'd shaved it in order to fit her with a catheter for the administration of drugs, drips or whatever they had to do before, during or after the operation.

Despite still being rather doped up from the effects of the anaesthetic, as soon as she saw me her tail wagged, slowly at first and then with more vigour as Rebecca placed her gently in my arms. Before going into the details regarding her treatment, Rebecca told me that the surgeon in Manchester had commented on how brave Sasha was, and that as they'd administered the anaesthetics to knock her out for the operation, her tail had continued wagging, getting slower and slower until she was fully under. Even more remarkable, he'd told Rebecca, was that as she began to come round in the recovery room the nurse who was with her reported to him that as consciousness began to return, that tail of hers had begun to wag, very slowly at first, and then by the time she'd woken up fully, it was wagging furiously. Despite all she'd gone through and even though she was still feeling the after-effects of the anaesthesia, Sasha's natural happiness, her verve and enthusiasm for life just shone through in that display of incessant tail wagging.

Next came the details of the operation itself. Rebecca explained that because Sasha was a mere ten weeks old, the surgeon had been very careful in terms of anaesthesia, giving her the bare minimum necessary dose, not wanting to add to the risks normally associated with anaesthetising an adult dog, which had also meant he'd had to work as fast and as accurately as possible. As she explained, the surgeon, whose name I can't recall, but will refer to as Mr. Burnside, was one of the best men in the north of England at doing these operations and he'd encountered no problems in completing Sasha's operation without any complications.

He'd used a series of screws and metal bolts in conjunction with an aluminium plate to rebuild Sasha's joint, which had been seriously damaged in the fall. It was going to take quite some time for her to recover and she would have to be kept in a dog crate and immobilised as much as possible until the joint was fully healed. All the time Rebecca was talking to me Sasha's tail was, yes, you've guessed it, wagging furiously as I cradled her in my arms.

"Keeping her immobilised will be the single most important factor in her recovery," she explained. "The quieter you can keep her, the quicker she'll heal. She can go out in the garden to go to the toilet, but you must try to keep her as still as possible. Rest is now the most important thing for Sasha."

"Thanks, Rebecca. It's going to be very difficult keeping an exuberant puppy cooped up for hours on end. How long will it be before she can walk on it, properly, I mean?"

"If all goes well, then maybe in two or three weeks the leg will be strong enough for her to have short periods of exercise, maybe ten minutes or so at a time in the garden."

"I'll do my best, Rebecca. We all just want her to be well again."

"I know you will, Mr. Porter. Let me go and get Sasha's tablets and then you can take her home."

Rebecca left me and Sasha while she went to fetch the medications, and while we waited, Sasha's eyes never left my face, the look she was giving me was pure love and devotion. Rebecca returned with the medications. She explained that Sasha had received a large dose of painkillers by injection so would need to begin taking the liquid painkilling medicine the next day, once in the morning, once at night, and she also had a course of antibiotics to help prevent any post-operative infection. I had to take her back for a post-operative check up in five days and after thanking Rebecca profusely, I carried Sasha to the car, where I gently placed her in the same wicker shopping basket I'd used to ferry her there in the first place just a couple of days before, though it seemed a lifetime ago at that moment.

Chapter 5

Post-operative Care

Juliet had prepared the dog crate for Sasha while I was out, but it took some time before the puppy saw the inside of it. Juliet of course insisted on giving her lots of love and cuddles, as did I, and the girls were allowed to stroke and pet her as one of us held her. Poor little dog was still so sleepy from the anaesthetic she just fell into a deep sleep within half an hour of coming home so we took the opportunity to place her in the dog crate in a special little bed I'd gone out and bought that fitted perfectly in the crate while still leaving her room to move around a little. The other dogs were all so interested in what was happening and all crowded round the crate. They could obviously smell 'vet' emanating from Sasha and we will always swear they knew Sasha wasn't well, as, after they'd sniffed at the crate and taken a good look at the sleeping little puppy they all left her alone to rest and not one dog made any attempt to disturb her.

A couple of hours later, Sasha woke up and as would become a habit over the coming weeks, I carried her into the back garden and placed her gently on the ground. It was quite heartrending to see her hobbling round on three legs, carefully ensuring she didn't put the injured, strapped up leg on the ground. How she did it, I'm still not sure, but somehow she managed to squat and do a little wee, and then limped to the bottom of the garden to the place where our dogs had all been trained to go to do their poo, Sasha included, even at that young age.

It must have been difficult for her to retain her balance but she did it and looked up at me as though to say "haven't I been clever?"

Not wanting her to do too much, I picked her up, and made such a fuss of her and then allowed her to spend the rest of the evening curled up in a blanket spread across my knees. This would become a feature of our evenings, with either me or Juliet having her with us in this way in order to reduce the amount of time she spent 'imprisoned' in her crate.

We'd tried offering her some food but as the vet had warned us, she was still quite drowsy and refused to eat. We hoped she'd feel hungry the next day.

Bedtime approached and once again I took her out into the garden and once again she 'performed' and hobbled back to me to be picked up and carried indoors.

All through that evening and every subsequent one during her convalescence, our other dogs were all superb, as if each one of them knew Sasha needed special care and not one displayed an ounce of jealousy such as we might have expected when dogs see another of their kind receiving extra special attention.

Thus began what was soon to become a regular ritual as I carried her crate upstairs and placed it beside our bed. Juliet brought Sasha upstairs in her arms and she was gently laid on her little bed in the bed where she soon fell fast asleep.

Just as had been the case before her accident, Sasha slept through the night, probably aided by the residual effects of the anaesthetic, and again, her crate was dry in the morning; no toilet accidents!

The following morning, we were so pleased when she appeared hungry and on being offered her usual breakfast, she eagerly lapped up the puppy food she'd now graduated to. In what would become quite a hallmark of Sasha's life, she readily swallowed her antibiotic tablet, wrapped in a little dog meat. To this day, Sasha, unlike some dogs, has never presented a problem in taking any form of medication. The painkilling Metacam was in liquid form and so administered by being mixed into her regular food, no problem!

At her first post-operative check-up at the vet's surgery, Rebecca expressed her pleasure at Sasha's progress and she carefully removed the full length bandage strapping her leg and I was able to see for the first time, the operation scars and stitches that still needed to be removed. Whilst the wound were healing well, it would be another week before the stitches could be removed but thankfully the leg was left unstrapped and it would at least make moving around a little easier for her.

* * *

We all settled into a new routine in our home which was basically one hundred percent Sasha related, as everything we did, everywhere either Juliet or I needed to go, had to be worked around the two of us giving our poor puppy what amounted to round the clock care and attention. The biggest problem we faced was that Sasha soon let us know, rather verbally, that she hated being left alone. She must have felt so isolated in her crate, where she had to spend most of her life over the following three months, toilet breaks and evening cuddles aside.

We'd thought that having her crate in the kitchen so the other dogs could 'visit' and be around her most of the time would help to alleviate her loneliness, but we soon learned that it wasn't canine company Sasha craved, but that of either her human 'Mum' or 'Dad' and she would whimper and howl in a plaintive, sad and sorry voice if neither of us was in the room with her.

Thankfully, for once, my own disabilities allowed us to come up with a workable solution. As I can't get around much anyway, we brought one of our garden chairs into the kitchen, where I could sit in relative comfort beside her crate. Result? Instant silence and a contended though still very much restricted puppy. I must have read upwards of a hundred books in those weeks sitting beside her, making sure she wasn't trying to move around too much as there was still a danger of her injuring herself as the joint healed.

My life and hers began to gradually meld into one as we began a routine of me sitting beside her, taking her out to go into the back garden, where she was soon able to spend gradually expanding periods of time out there, exercising her leg and gradually building up the strength in her rebuilt joint. From an initial five minutes or so, these periods grew to ten, then fifteen minutes, her limp gradually reducing, especially once her stitches had been removed. She received her second round of vaccinations during one of her regular check-ups and if it hadn't been for her accident, by now she would have been running around on the playing fields where we took our other dogs and enjoying the life of a fast-growing puppy.

Sadly, it wasn't to be for our little baby girl and it still strikes me as quite miraculous in light of subsequent events, that Sasha grew up as well-adjusted as she did. All those weeks when she should have been chasing balls, playing with squeaky toys, rolling around in the grass and play fighting with the other dogs, Sasha was cooped up in what was essentially a small cage, with usually just me for company, and with a couple of toys she could play with in that small enclosed space.

As her leg began to gain full strength however, I allowed her short periods of 'playtime' in the garden, which became therapeutic exercise periods and the vet eventually told me on one of her regular check-up visits that Sasha's leg had healed beautifully. A new set of x-rays were taken that showed everything was fine and three months after her horrific leg break, Sasha was given the all clear. The crate could be mothballed, hopefully never to be needed again.

She was cleared to go for walks, to run and play, and much to our joy we celebrated the fact that our beautiful little Sasha could be a real puppy at last. It was time for her to start enjoying her life again!

Chapter 6

Déjà Vu

The following two weeks were sheer joy for Sasha and all the family. We were able to take her out for walks, indulge in some basic dog training which she responded to as though she'd been taking secret lessons from Sheba or some of the other dogs in the home. We'd purchased a harness for her expecting her to be something of a 'puller' when out walking due to her not having had much chance to go for dog walks prior to her accident but she actually walked well and displayed a wonderfully happy, jaunty way of walking, with what could only be described as a big 'staffy grin' on her face as she virtually jogged along on her walks. We were so happy to be able to allow her to run free on the playing field near our home where she loved running and chasing a tennis ball, which she'd happily bring back to us without even being trained to do so. She loved simply running around and generally interacting with whichever dogs shared her walk. Of course, all the time she was running and enjoying herself; that tail of hers wagged and wagged and wagged.

In all honesty I can say that I'd never seen a dog, puppy or adult, display such a love of life as Sasha displayed in that period after she'd been given the all clear to resume normal life.

Our friends, many of whom were fellow dog owners, had missed seeing the little puppy we'd first shown them some months earlier, and expressed such delight in seeing her again and joined in our joy at seeing her displaying such happy puppy behaviour. Sasha truly brought immense smiles to so many faces and laughter too as they enjoyed her antics as she'd leap and run around, totally in love with life, almost oblivious to anything else happening around her.

Her home life was now that of a normal four month old puppy. She could play in the garden with the other dogs, climb the stairs at bedtime, though she was always a lot slower and rather careful on the way down, as she remains to this day. By now of course, she was eating the same diet as all our dogs and possessed a healthy appetite and was growing into a beautiful young dog, as fit and healthy as she could possibly be, taking into account the terrible start she'd experienced in life.

Being a multi-dog household it's worth explaining at this point that we have always used a series of baby gates in the home that allow us to ensure the dogs are where we want them to be at any given time. This arrangement has always worked well both before and after Sasha's arrival in our home but would play their part in the next event to strike our baby girl's fledgling puppyhood.

Just over two weeks had passed since Sasha had received the all-clear from the vet. One morning, Juliet was in the utility room, adjoining the kitchen, preparing to take three of our dogs out for a walk. Sasha must have sensed that Juliet was about to go out for a walk without taking her along.

Before either of us realised what was happening, Sasha decided to try and jump over the baby gate to try and reach Juliet, but didn't quite clear the top of the gate and fell awkwardly over the top, landing badly on the utility room side and crying out in pain as her right leg collapsed under her body. We realised right away what had happened and a quick look at the leg told us, without needing a definite diagnosis that she'd broken the leg yet again!

We could hardly believe it. Her right leg was once again sticking out at an impossible angle just as before. Sasha lay there looking up at me, wagging her tail as though nothing had happened, but both Juliet and I felt like breaking down in tears as we saw the leg, so recently healed, in that state once more.

Within minutes, after a phone call to the veterinary surgery, Sasha was once again on the passenger seat of the car as we sped along the road for immediate attention from the vet. This time she was too big to fit in the wicker basket so Juliet had quickly placed one of the dog beds on the seat and Sasha dutifully lay there, her right leg sticking out over the side all the way to the vets.

Less than twenty minutes after sustaining the new injury, she was being examined by an incredulous Rebecca, who as luck would have it, happened to be on duty at the time. Like Juliet and I she could hardly believe it.

"We'll need to x-ray the leg, Mr. Porter, but I'm ninety-nine percent sure she's broken the leg again in the same place."

"We couldn't believe it, Rebecca," I replied. "She's been so happy since you gave her the go ahead to live a normal life again."

Rebecca carefully made sure there were no other injuries immediately apparent and in a state of shock and with a terrible feeling of *déjà vu* I watched sadly as Rebecca carried Sasha through to the treatment area of the surgery where they would carry out the x-rays on her leg. Once again I was subjected to a pair of sad eyes watching me as I stood in the examination room as she disappeared from view. It was all happening again. My heart felt heavy, my emotions in turmoil as I walked out of the surgery and called Juliet from my mobile phone to give her the news she was already expecting. I drove home and as before, spent the next couple of hours nervously awaiting Rebecca's phone call.

Sure enough, when she called it was to confirm that Sasha's leg had indeed been broken in the same place, the elbow joint.

"Can you come back right away?" she asked me. "I've spoken to Mr. Burnside and if we can get Sasha across to Manchester this afternoon he can fit her in tomorrow. He stressed that the operation could be more complicated this time, as Sasha has grown significantly since the first one and he may have to remove the original plate and screws etc, and fit a new one in order to repair the damage if it's possible.

There is a slight chance, if the joint is too badly damaged to be repaired, that he may have to consider amputating the leg. The important thing for now is to get her over there so he can examine her thoroughly. If he needs to speak to you in the morning we can give him your number, with your permission."

"I'll be there right away," I replied, "and yes, of course you can give my phone number to Mr. Burnside. We just want Sasha to be okay."

The word 'amputation' resonated in my brain and both Juliet and I just looked at each other in shock after I'd briefly told her the gist of my conversation with Rebecca.

I was soon back in the surgery, signing yet another consent form for Sasha to be anaesthetised and operated on.

"Can I see her for a few minutes, Rebecca?" I asked.

"Of course you can. The pet ambulance won't be here for about twenty minutes. Just take your time. Sasha's a little dopey, from the sedative we had to give to take the x-rays, and from the strong dose of painkillers I've given her by injection."

I spent around ten minutes with Sasha before leaving her with that plaintive, pleading look in her eyes as she realised I was going away again without taking her with me. I felt like a mass murderer, but didn't want to be there to see her being driven away in the ambulance. That would have been too emotional for me. Sasha had become such an important part of my life and the lives of all the family. I could only drive home and yet again, the whole family sent an awful, worrisome evening and Juliet and I shared yet another sleepless night.

Our conversation during those sleepless hours mainly revolved around the potential prognoses for Sasha's future.

"What will we do if they have to amputate her leg?" Juliet had asked at one point.

"More's the point, what will Sasha do?" I replied. "Mind you, dogs can be very adaptable, and we've seen enough three-legged dogs over the years to know she would probably cope quite well if the worst case scenario happened."

"Let's hope the surgeon can re-build her joint again, so we don't have to worry about that option," Juliet replied, her voice tremulous with fear and emotion for Sasha.

"I agree. Hopefully, he'll call me in the morning and we'll know more then."

While it's true that many dogs cope admirably with three legs, we felt that Sasha was so young and vulnerable and had so far had such a little time to enjoy her puppyhood, that it was almost unthinkable for us to imagine our baby girl having to spend the rest of her life limping around on three legs.

* * *

Sure enough, quite early the following morning, my mobile phone rang. On answering it, I heard the voice of Mr. Burnside, the specialist veterinary orthopaedic surgeon who'd performed Sasha's operation on her original leg break.

"Well, Mr. Porter," he said in the calm and quiet voice I remembered from before. "Sasha certainly knows how to do things, doesn't she? Not content with once, she had to go and do it again, eh?"

"I know, Mr. Burnside. My wife and I just couldn't believe she'd done it again. The baby gate is three feet high and God knows how she thought she could jump something that tall."

"Typical puppy behaviour," he replied. "Inquisitive and adventurous to a fault, though I have to admit, in all my years as a vet, I have never known a dog break the same leg in the same place twice in the space of four months."

"Yes, I can imagine it's a rare occurrence, but please, is there anything you can do to save the leg?"

"I think so," he said, and a sense of relief instantly washed over me, even at the hint of being able to save her from amputation. He continued; "However, I must point out that this time the operation will be rather more complicated than the previous one. Because Sasha has grown considerably, there's no chance of using the original plate and pins etcetera to repair the joint so I'll have to open her leg up and first of all remove all the previous inserts and then put in place a new, larger metal plate, with correspondingly larger pins and screws to hold it in place. I have to point out that this involves quite a bit of reconstructive work and it's fair to say that if she does manage to somehow do this again in the future, it will be almost impossible to save the leg and amputation would then become a necessity in order to give her a decent quality of life."

Mr. Burnside checked that I fully understood his words and the possible implications for Sasha's future, and then promised to phone me personally later in the day when the operation had been completed.

I thanked him and wished him good luck with Sasha's operation and before he hung up he did add; "I will do everything I can for Sasha, Mr. Porter. She does seem to be a very special dog. Not that I can put my finger on why, it's just something that comes across to me while interacting with her. Please try not to worry. She's in safe hands, I assure you."

I think that was the first time anyone had referred to Sasha as being a 'special dog,' a sentiment I agreed with of course, but then again, I was biased. With the progression of time, it certainly wouldn't be the last time such a phrase would be used in people's descriptions of my baby girl.

The hours that followed became a sort of 'groundhog day' experience for Juliet and me as we relived all the fears and worries that had beset us during Sasha's first operation such a few short months previously. After walking the dogs, we did our best to keep busy by retrieving the dog crate from its place of storage in the garden shed, and Juliet once again prepared it to make it as comfortable as possible in readiness for Sasha's homecoming. I had to go out that morning to buy our regular two large sacks of dog food, which would usually last our 'pack' around two and half weeks. While I was at the pet food superstore, where I was a well known regular customer, I told the staff who all knew Sasha after she'd paid numerous visits there with me of her latest injury and all of them wished her luck and offered their best wishes for her speedy recovery. While I was there I bought her a new, soft cuddly toy, a little puppy she could snuggle up to in her crate at night.

There was little more we could do but wait for the promised phone call from the orthopaedic surgeon. Eventually, at around one p.m. Mr. Burnside called me.

"Sasha's fine," were his first words to me and relief spread through my tensed up body before he said another word. "It was a long operation, over three hours, but we were successful in removing the previous internal supports and fitting the new plate, bolts and screws. It will be necessary for her to be kept as immobile as possible as before, but she should make a full recovery."

"Thank you," I said, my voice choked with emotion.

"It's a pleasure," he replied "and my nurses have asked me to tell you that Sasha has an incredible tail."

"Really?"

"Yes," he said with a slight hint of humour in his voice. "Just like the first time, her tail continued wagging as she went under the anaesthetic, slower and slower until she was fast asleep and as she was waking up it was like a machine being switched back on as it gradually began wagging again, getting faster and faster until she was fully awake."

"That's my Sasha," I said, "always happy, no matter what."

We shared a laugh, a welcome moment in the midst of a very serious situation.

He went on to explain the full details of the operation and ended by telling me they would be transporting Sasha back to my own vet's surgery within the hour, and that my vet would call me as soon as it was possible for me to collect her and take her home.

That call came around five thirty p.m and soon afterwards, I arrived once more at the surgery. Sasha's leg was once again strapped up from toe to shoulder and true to form, her tail wagged furiously as Rebecca brought her into the consulting room and she caught sight of me. After another lecture on the after care required for my baby girl, and armed with more liquid painkiller and antibiotics, we journeyed home where Sasha received a rapturous welcome from Juliet and the girls.

The next few weeks were very much a repetition of what had gone before, with the garden chair again being employed as I kept my usual daily vigil by her side and my reading increased once again to take in novel after novel, with an occasional factual historical volume thrown in for good measure. Once again she would spend the evenings either on Juliet's knee or on mine, and her only exercise consisted of her short trips in the garden for toileting at first and then for actual exercise periods as her leg gained more strength.

Probably because we'd gained such valuable experience in 'managing' Sasha's condition from the previous instance, this time her convalescence and recovery seemed to go far more smoothly and we soon settled into the routine and the regime we'd instituted previously.

Because she'd grown considerably since breaking her leg the first time it did however prove a little more difficult to keep her 'quiet and immobile' this time round, and it was evident from her behaviour that Sasha wanted to be out of the crate and back in the swing of things much sooner than before. Thankfully she proved a fast healer yet again and after regular trips to the vet for check-ups and with gradually increasing exercise periods in the garden helping her leg to gain strength, it seemed to us that the time passed much faster this time. Sasha had become adept at walking in such a way that she put minimum weight on her leg as she placed it on the ground and almost miraculously, even with the strapping still in place for a longer period than previously, she actually tried to start playing with the other dogs when they were allowed in the garden with her. We felt it the right thing to do to allow her (and them) to carry on as normally as possible during this second period of recovery and convalescence. I'm sure it helped both her physical and psychological recovery to enjoy that degree of normality with the other dogs. The last thing we needed at that time was a depressed dog, something that could easily have happened without sufficient mental and physical stimulation.

Despite the greater complexity of the second operation, Sasha's quite remarkable ability to heal herself saw her receive the all-clear just ten weeks after undergoing surgery, a full two weeks less than the first time.

This time we made sure she was given no opportunity to repeat her previous performance of trying to jump over the baby gate, keeping her under very close supervision at all times as she began to enjoy her much delayed puppyhood once again. It was quite incredible to realise that though she was now eight months old, she had sent almost five of those months as a virtual prisoner in her crate, all for the best possible reasons of course, but she really did have a lot of exploring, playing and general life experiences to catch up with.

Over the following months we made sure she had every opportunity to indulge in every pleasurable experience we could provide her with, interrupted only by one more experience of surgery as Rebecca, her vet had recommended that we have Sasha neutered at the earliest time possible. This time, the short operation was carried out by Rebecca at our local surgery and Sasha was admitted and returned to us within the space of one day. Sasha had become so used to visiting the veterinary surgery by this time that when we walked in together early in the morning she automatically tried to walk through into the main treatment area before waiting to go through the usual admissions process.

One of the veterinary nurses later told me Sasha was the 'perfect' patient, as she seemed to know the procedures involved in terms of pre-op medications, having her leg shaved for the insertion of the catheter, and just like at Manchester, the staff at my own surgery commented on her wagging tail while going under and during the waking process. Rebecca, who had seen Sasha probably more frequently than any of her other patients in the last six months became the next person to remark to me, when I went to collect her, that there was 'something special' about Sasha.

As we enjoyed her development over the next few months, we were yet to discover just how 'special' our lovable Sasha really was. Her first birthday came and went, (we'd given her a birth date based on the approximate age at which she'd been found by the dog warden, and going back eight weeks from that date), and life was at last looking up for Sasha. She was happy, playful and everyone who met her when she was out walking or playing on the nearby field remarked on what a beautiful dog she was growing into.

Whether it was running free on the field chasing her ball, or just play fighting or running around with the other dogs, Sasha seemed to be making up for lost time, literally by leaps and bounds, (excuse the analogy), and everything in the garden of her life looked rosy.

Chapter 7

Good Times, Bad Times

By the time Sasha's leg was fully healed, autumn had crept up on us and the weather, though still warm and sunny for the most part, had turned changeable, so much so that for the first time, Sasha's nemesis suddenly reared its head during a particularly unsettled weather week. Though we hadn't really taken much notice of it previously, occasionally thinking she might not want to go out for a walk if she was suffering some residual pain in her joint perhaps, we now found out the true reason for her periodic reticence to leave the house…RAIN!

Sasha absolutely hated getting wet. Every time we tried to take her for a walk in the rain, and that week we had rain every day, we'd get as far as the tall, five foot gate that led from just outside our back door to the garden path and the outside world, and she'd dig her heels in and refuse to go any further. We tried and we tried, first Juliet, then me, all to no avail. We'd have to wait until a break in the rain and then try to take her for a walk in the hope it stayed dry long enough to give her the exercise she needed. If it began to rain while out walking with her, she was intelligent enough to know digging her heels in would only cause her to get even wetter, so her tactic in that case was to simply turn in the direction of home and literally drag the unfortunate walker along the path at the best speed she could muster, bearing in mind one of us was hanging on to her lead for dear life!

To this day, she simply will not go for a walk in the rain, though she has gradually deemed it acceptable, over the years, to go for a very short one in the lightest of drizzle. So just when you were all thinking we had this wonderful, perfect amazing dog, I've gone and shattered your illusions haven't I? Even our wonderful Sasha has her idiosyncrasies, with rain being right at the top of her list of 'pet hates' (excuse the pun).

Rain aside, Sasha was loving life, living it to the full at long last and sharing time with her was a sheer joy. She was certainly growing into an extremely good looking dog, and drew admiring comments from many people we met while out walking with her. It was while she was playing with two of our other dogs on the playing field one day that we discovered yet another of those idiosyncrasies; small fluffy dogs! If Sasha saw a small fluffy dog, for example a Shih Tzu or Maltese terrier, she'd immediately make a bee line for it. At first we thought she was going to actually attack such dogs, but then we discovered she thought they were large dog toys! Seriously she would run up to them, bowl them over, start leaping around like a demented, whirling dervish, or to be more accurate and precise, like a very large overgrown puppy. Of course, most dog owners who didn't know Sasha understandably found her behaviour rather scary and they too believed their dogs to be under attack by this rampaging 'monster' that would come running across the field towards their poor little darlings. We soon realised we'd have to keep Sasha on her lead if small fluffy dogs were around, and still have to do that today. She's now a full grown Staffy of course and strong enough to knock almost any dog down if she runs into it like a battering ram at full speed.

In fact, her antics with small fluffy dogs tended to mirror certain be-haviour at home, where she has always been rather... let's say, clumsy. If she wants to get from A to B, Sasha tends to be quite single minded about it and will often almost knock me or Juliet down as she clumps past us, banging into our legs in her determination to get where she wants to be. Over the years, she's walked into doors, chair legs, and even an occasional wall. 'Bull in a china shop' would be an apt description of Sasha on a mission! Or should that be 'Bull terrier in a china shop?'

As most of the current staff at Sasha's veterinary practice can testify, Sasha can be so excitable when I take her in for regular check-ups that she howls if she sees other dogs in the waiting room, so I usually wait outside until it's her turn to be seen.

But, to return to our story, life for Sasha had now become just what it should have been from the beginning. It was not long after her first birthday however, that we noticed she was continually licking at the pad of one of her front paws. At first, thinking it was a minor irritation caused by walking in something on the field or something picked up during a walk, we didn't give it too much attention but as the days turned to two weeks with no sign of the problem going away, I once again made a phone call and arranged an appointment for Sasha to see the vet.

The following day, we arrived for her appointment nice and early. Luckily, we were met with an empty surgery, no dogs for her to howl at.

Rebecca examined her paws and after seeing or sensing something we hadn't seen or identified she moved on to examine the inside of her ears. After completing her examination, as Sasha stood wagging her tail as usual, Rebecca announced her belief that Sasha was suffering from a type of canine dermatitis. If her diagnosis was correct, she explained, this was a form of the disease that affected the pads and skin of the inner ears, in other words, the exposed bare skin areas and was more prevalent in white dogs than those of other colours. It had to happen to Sasha of course, didn't it? She prescribed antihistamine tablets and we hoped it would soon clear the problem, but, in true Sasha style, it didn't. After trying for a month to eradicate the infection, Rebecca decided to take blood samples from Sasha to be sent to the lab for testing, in the hope they may be able to identify the cause of any allergy that may be at the root of the problem.

Sure enough, a couple of allergies were found after the blood samples were tested. First of all, Sasha was found to be allergic to the almost microscopic 'food mites' found in the dust present in all dried proprietary dog foods. As Sasha was fed on the same dried food as the rest of our dogs, with a little meat added to the evening meal, this came as a surprise as none of our other dogs had ever exhibited any such symptoms. It had to be Sasha of course! It also appeared she had a lesser allergy to certain grass seeds which it would be almost impossible to prevent her coming into contact with.

It was possible, however, for us to take action to help prevent her coming into contact with the mites in the food dust. Quite simply, Rebecca advised a change of food, something different from the dried food she was used to. As a result we changed her food to a soft food, not tinned meat, but one that came in sealed bags that helped maintain its moist contents. She now had her own special diet while the other dogs remained on the dry food. This, together with daily steroid tablets helped to bring the problem under control to some extent. Unfortunately, this problem has remained with her since that time and she has to take the tablets permanently, which we have to increase at times when the allergy flares up, as it does from time to time. It's a shame and quite upsetting to see her scratching her ears and licking and chewing at her pads when the allergy decides to show itself, but Sasha, being Sasha, just gets on with life, without letting the irritation affect her enjoyment of each day.

So, after surviving her initial abandonment, followed by two broken legs, well, one leg broken twice, our baby girl now found herself with something else to contend with. A human being might fall into mega depression as a result of all the setbacks she suffered in those first two years, but not Sasha. We were by now beginning to realise just how resilient, resourceful and 'special' our beautiful rescued staffy was.

Chapter 8

Best Friend, Sheba

I think this is a good point in Sasha's 'tale' to tell you about her very best doggie pal, what we humans might refer to as her BFF. As she approached two years of age, it was apparent that she and Sheba had formed a strong bond with one another.

Like Sasha, Sheba is a Staffordshire bull terrier, a brindle-coloured girl who, though aged almost ten now, compared with Sasha's five and a half, is considerably smaller than Sasha. Another rescue dog, Sheba represents the worst case of dog abuse it has been our misfortune to encounter in all our years of keeping rescue dogs. Her story is quite heart-rending.

On one of our regular visits to the dog pound, as we looked at the various dogs currently offered for adoption, we came across a pathetic sight in a separate area, not usually open to the public. As regular adopters from the pound we were allowed to wander wherever we wanted in those days.

There, in a small stall, curled up in a foetal position and with a heat lamp suspended from the ceiling overhead, we saw the most pathetic sight imaginable. We both immediately filled up with tears at the sight of the poor creature that lay shivering under that lamp.

We immediately went and asked the staff for the dog's story. Apparently the dog had been used as bait, for training fighting dogs and when she was no longer of use to her so-called owner, she'd been thrown on a rubbish tip and left to die.

An anonymous tip to the local dog warden service had informed them that a dog had been left on a council rubbish disposal site at a specified location and the informant ended the call by saying, "I think it's still alive." They could only assume that a member of the owner's family or perhaps a neighbour had made the call out of a sense of guilt or an attack of conscience.

I was later able to speak to the warden who'd been dispatched to check out the tip-off and she had found the dog, barely alive and immediately taken her to the dog pound where a vet was summoned and due to the nature of her injuries and poor health the possibility of putting the unfortunate dog to sleep had been considered but the staff at the pound, well-aware of what must have been done to her, pleaded with the vet to try and save her. The vet agreed and the undernourished, skeletal and very sick dog was put on a drip, given fluids, her many wounds treated, and given antibiotics and other necessary medications. She was hardly able to eat and at first they'd had to feed her intravenously as she was unable to take solid foods. By the time we saw her, she'd been in the pound for three weeks and still looked a terrible and upsetting sight.

In short, she had virtually no fur, just grey skin covered in bite marks and other wounds, had ligature marks round her neck where she'd obviously been tied up so the fighters could get at her; she was horrendously underweight to the extent that every bone in her body was visible through her skin and she was, in fact, little more than a living skeleton. From the shape of her head and body configuration, the vet had assessed her as being a Staffy, though it took quite a stretch of the imagination at that point to see it. He'd put her age at around one year old or less, and the thoughts of the life she'd led as a puppy caused both Juliet and I to fill up with tears. *Who on earth could treat a living, breathing, naturally loving animal like this?*

Sadly, we all knew the answer only too well. Because of their (wholly undeserved) reputation, many Staffordshire Bull Terriers were, (and still are) used by a certain section of the population in illegal dog-fighting, as well as being trained as 'weapon dogs' by criminals and other generally anti-social members of our society.

The Staffy is in general a wonderful loving dog when brought up and raised properly, as with any breed. In fact, few people are aware that the breed actually features near the top of a list complied by The Kennel Club of Great Britain of ideal family dogs. Staffies were actually known as the 'nanny dog' by the Victorians who would often use the breed as 'baby sitters,' being trusted to guard and look after their children.

Juliet and I have been privileged to own and love a number of Staffies over the years, and can certainly testify to their loving nature and their desire to please their owners. Adverse publicity has meant that even today, people will often cross the street if they see a Staffy coming towards them. In fact, statistics provided by the R.S.P.C.A. (The Royal Society for the prevention of cruelty to animals), show that the dog breed recorded as having committed the most attacks on humans is in fact the much-loved Labrador!

So, back to Sheba. As Juliet and I stood looking down at her, we'd both been sharing the same thoughts. *Was there anything we could do for this poor dog?*

Probably because they knew us so well and were aware of our love and commitment to rescue dogs, the owners of the dog pound came to a decision when we enquired about the poor miserable little bundle shivering in that cold stall. The heat lamp helped, but there was no central heating for the canine residents at the pound and a chill wind was blowing through the buildings, adding winter's chill to everyone and everything. The owner made us an offer.

"If you think you can give her a good home and some love and happiness in whatever time she has left, we'll waive the usual adoption fee and paperwork and you can take her home with you and do whatever you can for her. She was probably the runt of a litter, and has in all probability never known any home life at all. All she's known is cruelty and pain. Are you prepared to take her knowing she might not live long?"

The usual fee for adopting a dog from the pound at that time was £110, around $170 at today's exchange rates. For them to forego that fee was a sure sign of the fact that they didn't expect the little dog to live long, such was the terrible state of her health and overall condition, and also the trust and faith they had in Juliet and I to give her the best life possible in her remaining life.

Despite the fact we might not have her for long and were potentially putting ourselves in the firing line for eventual heartbreak, we didn't hesitate. As we used to take our dogs in the car regularly the rear section of our estate car was fitted out with a large quilted dog mattress and we always had a plentiful supply of towels in the car for cleaning muddy paws etc, so within five minutes, we had wrapped the little dog in a couple of warm dry towels and placed her gently on the mattress in the back of the car.

By the time we arrived home we'd decided to name her Sheba, a regal name for the sad, sick little dog. From that day forward she'd be treated like the queen who once bore that name. She'd never need to be afraid again. When we pulled up outside our home we received a shock as we lifted the tailgate. The rear compartment of the car was covered in blood! Sheba was sitting there looking nervously at us as she wagged her tail at us. We soon realised that the staff at the pound had forgotten to tell us that because of the starvation she'd suffered at the hands of her original owner, Sheba had been reduced to twisting round and trying to eat her own tail! On examination, we could now see that the rear half of her tail was little more than a bloody mess. She must have felt so happy in the back of the car, perhaps sensing the love we'd already shown her in that short tine at the pound that she must have sat there wagging her tail and spraying blood everywhere as we drove along.

"Oh well, it's only blood," Juliet said. "We can clean it up later. Let's get her inside for now, but you'll need to take her to the vet as soon as possible to have her tail looked at."

We carried Sheba into the house and placed her on the floor in the kitchen. Our other dogs instantly gathered round her to take a look at the new arrival. Now, one advantage of living with a number of dogs is that it has given us the unique opportunity to observe 'pack behaviour' in a way that most dog owners never get a chance to see.

Sheba sat on the kitchen floor, trembling with fear as our dogs approached her, possibly expecting that they were going to attack her. After all, that was her experience of other dogs up to that point in her life, so who could blame her for such a reaction? When she stood up, her front legs could hardly support her, and they were bent at an unusual angle from the malnutrition she'd suffered.

What followed was quite amazing and very touching. It was as if our dogs sensed the fear and the vulnerability in Sheba, not in an aggressive way, but rather that they could tell she'd been abused, tortured and badly neglected. Instead of the usual excitement they would usually display at a new addition to the family, they held back, and slowly, just one or two at a time, they ventured closer to her, and after wagging their tails at her in a friendly manner, they simply walked away, back to their own beds or out into the garden. It was a surreal moment really, seeing and realising that the so-called canine 'sixth sense' probably had some basis in fact. They just knew Sheba needed help, and peace and quiet, and they automatically granted her just that.

Juliet did her best to stem the flow of blood from her tail while I made a phone call to the vet and after I explained the circumstances they agreed to see her straight away.

Bernard was the vet who was on duty that afternoon and he examined Sheba thoroughly. He agreed she was very weak, but after I'd told him what she'd gone through in her short life, he became as determined as we were to do all he could for her. Vets tend to hate cruelty to animals even more than the average person. After all they're the ones who are left with treating the aftermath of such treatment, and so Sheba became a sort of 'pet project' for Bernard. Between us, we were going to give Sheba a full and happy life.

First of all, we had to treat her tail. Bernard prescribed a cream that I would have to apply four times a day. It was, he explained, a very strong medication and had to be applied wearing surgical gloves, and he gave me a supply to keep me going until I could buy some. If we couldn't stop the bleeding, it might transpire that he'd have to amputate part of her tail, but for now we'd do our best to save it.

He also recommended a diet that would help to gradually build her strength up again. Due to the state of malnutrition she'd suffered it wasn't possible to put her onto a normal diet right away. The surgery sold all the various special dietary products and so I was able to take a supply home with me, along with the cream for her tail. While we were there, he also gave her the first half of her inoculations. Sheba's rehabilitation had begun.

Over the next couple of weeks, I scrupulously applied the cream to her tail, four times a day as prescribed. It must have stung incredibly because, as I applied it, she would wince and close her eyes, much as we would when experiencing a sharp pain. I found it incredible that despite the pain it must have caused her, never once did Sheba try to turn and snap at me for causing her that pain. To this day I swear that the poor dog somehow knew I was trying to help her and that the cream was an essential part of that help. I would call her and she'd come to me and sit patiently as I spoke softly to her and applied the cream, then wagged her tail in anticipation as I removed the gloves and rewarded her with a treat, one of her favourite dog biscuits.

Miraculously, the tail began to heal and at the end of the two week course, the cream had done its job. Bernard the vet was delighted. We'd saved Sheba's tail. Not only that, but she'd started to gain weight too. When I'd first taken her to the vet, she'd weighed no more than six kilograms, less than half the average weight of a typical one year old Staffy. Now, Sheba began to grow into a beautiful dog, her brindle fur started to grow again and her skeletal frame began to fill out. She hated rain, for different reasons to Sasha though, as it seemed to sting and burn her skin before her fur grew back, and even today, she's a little nervous of going out when it's wet.

All things considered, Sheba was lucky, far luckier than many other dogs forced to endure the torture and torment she went through. When Sasha came into her life, Sheba instantly seemed to attach herself to Sasha and the two became the best of friends. They play together, go for walks together and despite the fact that she's the older of the two dogs, Sheba definitely seems to depend on Sasha, to feel secure when Sasha's close by, and the only thing that scares Sheba nowadays, apart from other dogs out on the street who she still thinks are going to attack her, is the sound of fireworks exploding, or other loud banging noises.

As I said at the start of this chapter, I thought it was time you knew Sasha's best friend. Now you know why.

Chapter 9

The Puppies

Still in her second year, Sasha was soon to display yet another amazing talent. In the autumn, we decided we'd like to have a puppy around the house.

Seeing an advertisement in the local paper, we went along to visit a family who were selling a litter of Staffy/Springer Spaniel pups. They were all gorgeous puppies and the couple owned the mother who we met as well. Juliet wanted the little black one with a white chest, I wanted the black and white one with beautiful markings. I gave in and we reserved the little black one with a deposit. Next morning, I surprised Juliet by going to collect the puppy and coming home with two! I couldn't come away without the black and white little girl too.

We named the sisters Muffin (the black one) and Petal, both of whom settled in immediately, hardly surprising as we soon saw they appeared to have a new Mum. Seeing the two puppies lying together in a dog bed, Sasha had got in the bed with them and was proudly sitting over the two sleeping puppies as though she was a mother guarding her own pups. From that day forwards, Muffin and Petal have always slept with Sasha and still seem to regard her as a mother figure. Two weeks after we got the two sisters the lady we'd bought them from phoned to ask if we'd like the last of the litter, a little boy pup. Apparently her husband had gone to deliver it to a couple the day before but took one look at the home and family and refused to handover the puppy. He didn't like the look of the place or the attitude of the people. What a responsible owner! When I explained that we couldn't afford a third puppy the lady said she and her husband had talked it over and both of them thought we were a loving, caring couple who could give the dog a good home and they were prepared to let us have the last puppy for a nominal amount.

Off I went in the car, returning an hour later with Muffin and Petal's brother who we named Digby. Sasha had another pup to look after and she duly took Digby under her wing as well as the two girls. It was so touching to see her caring for those little eight week old pups as though she really was their natural mother. Digby, coming along a couple of weeks later was never quite as close to Sasha as the other two, but there's a definite bond between her and the three puppies, who are now approaching their fourth birthday. The three of them have grown up together from birth and we always describe them as being like one dog with twelve legs because they do everything together, If Muffin goes into the garden, the others go too. If one comes to sit on the sofa with Juliet, the other two have to be included too. Of course, 'Mummy' Sasha is still always around keeping an eye on things, and will often sit in the garden watching the three of them playing together as though she's supervising them. Great to see!

The other advantage of having the three together was that they all seemed to learn from each other and toilet training was a breeze. Once we'd pointed them in the right direction and showed them where they were supposed to 'go' they all just followed one another and we barely had a single 'accident' in the home. Again, they would also follow Sasha when she went in the garden and most of the time would copy her if she went to do a pee, or the other!

Once we started taking the pups out for walks, people automatically asked if they were Sasha's, probably due to the similar colour and markings on Petal in particular, who could very easily be taken for Sasha's natural offspring. Muffin in mostly black as I previously explained whilst Digby is a mixed brindle and white colour, his head being white with a brindle patch over one eye, a very cute looking dog.

So, along with all her other attributes, we could now add 'surrogate mother' to Sasha's list. She really was proving to be a very special dog.

Chapter 10

Fit

Sasha, the puppies, Sheba, and our other dogs, Dexter, Penny, Cassie, Dylan and Muttley, along with the human side of the family were now enjoying what we thought was a happy and fairly active life together, the dogs of course always providing a sense of fun to each day.

Sasha was now two and a half years old and apart from the scars on her upper leg from her two operations, we had all happily put the awful traumas of her first year a long way behind us. She still had to take the tablets to help with her skin allergies, but in every other aspect of life she was fit and healthy, or, so we thought.

Early one morning at around five a.m. Sasha had woken me as sometimes happened, needing to go outside. I donned my dressing gown and took her downstairs, opened the back door and she went out as usual. She trotted back into the house a couple of minutes later and instead of going though the utility room into the kitchen to wait for me to lock up so we could go back to bed, she stood looking up at me and wouldn't move. She just didn't look 'right.'

"Sasha, come on, let's go back to bed," I said, trying to encourage her to go back upstairs with me.

Before I knew what was happening, her face seemed to contort, her legs began to shake and Sasha suddenly fell over onto her side. Her legs began moving as though she was running at top speed, and the most terrible sound came from deep in her throat, a howling sound

I had never heard in my life. She was foaming at the mouth and she lost control of her bladder.

Not sure what was taking place, I shouted upstairs to Juliet.

"Juliet, come quickly. Sasha's having some kind of fit or something."

Knowing I wasn't one to panic unduly, Juliet came running down the stairs and joined me in the utility room where I was now on my knees at Sasha's side. The other dogs who slept in the kitchen were all agitated and trying to see what was happening but I'd closed the baby gate separating the kitchen from the utility room so they couldn't interfere with whatever was happening.

"What happened?" Juliet asked.

"I don't know. She just went out as normal and came back in and collapsed."

As I spoke, Sasha's movements began to slow down, her legs finally returning to rest, and the noise in her throat finally fell silent. She continued lying there for another five minutes or so, during which time Juliet sat on the floor and cradled Sasha's head on her lap, slowly and gently stroking her head, crying for our baby girl, who we both thought might have suffered a stroke. To have had to witness our poor Sasha in the grip of the seizure, her legs threshing about, her terrible howling and uncontrollable jerking body movements was enough to bring us both to tears, which we both unashamedly cried, believing something very serious had just taken place.

After another few minutes, Sasha began to 'come round' and though I tried talking to her, she seemed unaware of my presence for a couple of minutes. As suddenly as it began, the 'incident' was over as Sasha suddenly seemed to 'snap out of it' and as if nothing had happened, she rose to her feet and began walking through to the kitchen. It was a weird sensation as if what had taken place had been nothing more than a 'blip' or a minor interruption to her walking back in from the garden.

"What the hell was that?" I said to no-one in particular.

Juliet was now standing, watching as Sasha wandered happily across the kitchen to the hallway door, waiting to go back to bed.

While I took our beautiful but obviously very poorly dog back upstairs to her bed, Juliet stayed downstairs to clear up after the seizure.

* * *

For once, I didn't bother making an appointment at the vets. I was waiting at the doors with Sasha in the car as they opened up at 8.15 that morning. The reception staff could tell by my face that something serious had happened, and as usual, they all made a big fuss of Sasha. They quickly had me admitted to see Rebecca who took only a few minutes of talking to me to come to the conclusion that Sasha had suffered an epileptic fit. After all she'd suffered already in her life, now she had something new to contend with.

"Surely she's too young to have contracted something like that," I said in a mood of naïve denial of the facts, trying perhaps to make it go away by not believing in the truth of the situation.

"It usually strikes dogs anywhere from the age of two and a half to three years old," Rebecca told me, and of course, Sasha was exactly two and a half.

Rebecca immediately started Sasha on a course of medications, two separate tablets that she had to take each day and over the next couple of weeks a series of tests proved beyond doubt that our baby girl had indeed fallen foul of this most insidious illness. I already had a cousin who had suffered from epilepsy for many years and I had seen at first hand what a terrible effect the condition can have on a person's life. I could only hope it wouldn't affect my Sasha as badly as it had my cousin, Brenda.

We had no idea if or when the next seizure might occur. Rebecca had told me that often there can be a period of months between seizures, sometimes only weeks. In Sasha's case unfortunately, we didn't have long to wait.

Less than four weeks later, Sasha keeled over again whilst in the midst of eating her breakfast. She recovered quite quickly, and we thought that was the end of it for that day. We were wrong. Over the following couple of hours she had two more seizures, all of short duration, but all so distressing to witness. It was time to see the vet once again.

Now it appeared that Sasha was prone to what were called 'cluster seizures' whereby the dog could suffer from two, three, sometimes four seizures in rapid succession. The vet now added diazepam to her list of medications. This came in small applicators that had to be administered rectally at the time of a seizure, the intention being to relax the brainwaves in order to prevent further seizure activity.

Months went by with no let up in the cluster seizures, Sasha often suffering from four in rapid succession. We could do nothing for her during a seizure, apart from making sure she didn't hurt herself in her unconscious thrashing around, and we'd never felt so helpless. In time, new medications were tried in an attempt to bring the condition under better control and then, much to my disappointment I learned that Rebecca had been taken ill and would be taking a long period of rest from work.

As she'd been Sasha's vet since the time of her first ever visit to the practice and knew her condition better than anybody, I worried about Sasha's future care and treatment. I soon found my worries to be groundless.

In the midst of Sasha's early months of suffering from epilepsy I had cause to visit the surgery with Petal who had developed a serious limp in one of her front legs. The vet who treated her was new to the practice, and Ben immediately fell in love with Petal, describing her as one of the most beautiful dogs he'd ever met. With her breeding of half staffy/half springer spaniel, Petal had grown to be an impressive looking dog. She still had the beautiful markings that had first caught my attention, but she now had a long and expressive tail, fur as soft as a spaniel's, and the feature that most appealed to Ben, the most expressive eyes you could imagine with big white eyelashes.

Over the next few weeks, as he treated her problem, Ben had the leg x-rayed and we discovered that Petal was suffering from elbow dysplasia, a potentially crippling condition. Thankfully, with lots of care and attention and the correct medications, we were able to ease the pain in her leg and after further x-rays Ben assured us that Petal didn't have the condition in as serious a form as she might have had. In time, she might even grow out of it as she was still a young dog. Over the years since then, apart from the occasional flare-up of the condition, Petal has remained pain-free and loves nothing better than getting out onto the playing field and running about and playing with lots of rough and tumble games with her brother and sister. The three puppies as we still refer to them, really are totally inseparable.

* * *

Soon after Petal's problem had been treated, Ben experienced his first exposure to the charms of Sasha. Well, if his meeting Petal had been 'love at first sight' his first encounter with Sasha was like a case of *Déjà vu*. Sasha of course worked her charms on Ben and as always, she proved totally irresistible. This was the time when I learned that Ben had also owned an epi-dog, a term a lot of owners of epileptic dogs use to describe their pets.

This turned out to be a case of happy serendipity, as Ben explained that he'd made it a priority in his life as a vet to research and study the treatments available for epileptic dogs, originally as a means of helping his own dog, but of course he was now in a position to share his experience and knowledge of the illness with the owners of other sufferers.

Having reviewed the history of Sasha's illness, Ben suggested a change to her medication. I was happy to agree if it would help her and he contacted Rebecca, who it transpired was still in daily contact with the practice despite her own illness, to ensure she was in agreement with him amending her treatment plan. She was happy to go along with his proposal and so Sasha began a new course of tablets, plus having the dose of her Phenobarbital increased. She now had Li-bromide added to her drug regime in addition to the Aktivait tablets, a herbal medication that was designed to help in reducing excessive brain activity. She still needed the Diazepam of course to be administered immediately a seizure occurred, but now Ben advised me it was okay for me to double the current dosage if she suffered a second or subsequent attack, or if the first one didn't appear to be helping in the case of any single fit.

For a while, Sasha continued to suffer from cluster fits, though the periods between attacks gradually increased slightly, from an average interval of every three weeks to four, not much admittedly, but at that point even a small improvement was welcome.

Could life throw anything more at my beautiful little Sasha? I could only take a pragmatic view and hope for the best.

Chapter 11

Research & Reactions

It's a feature of canine epilepsy that in between seizures, the dog acts completely normally and is able to go about life pretty much as usual. As the realisation slowly dawned on Juliet and I that Sasha was going to be affected by the epilepsy for life, I decided to find out as much as I could about the illness and when I began an internet search I unearthed a number of facts that I hadn't previously considered.

Apparently, when in the grip of a seizure, the dog loses certain senses. This explained certain things to us. We now knew for example that though Sasha was moving around madly while 'fitting' she was to all intents and purposes in an unconscious state and was unable to hear us when we tried to reassure and love her. Worst of all, when 'coming out' of the seizure, Sasha was actually blind for a time, until she was fully in recovery mode. This explained her seeming inability to recognise us until she'd recovered, as not only couldn't she hear us, but she couldn't see us and would therefore be totally disorientated for a short time.

"That's just terrible for her," Juliet commented as I revealed the results of my quick research.

"I know," I replied. "It must be so frightening for her to come round and feel totally out of control of her senses like that. No wonder she's so extra loving and needy when she finally cones out of a seizure."

That statement was so true, as when she recovered from a seizure, Sasha's first instinct was to come to me and either lean her head on my leg, or sit on my foot, the contact seeming to give her a measure of reassurance. I, in turn would always make sure I gave her lots of love and attention to make her feel secure and loved.

My research had also revealed that the dog would actually have no recollection of what had happened during a seizure, hence the often almost comical times when Sasha would suddenly begin fitting while eating her breakfast for example, causing us to be so concerned and upset for her, and then would recover, stand up and promptly carry on eating her breakfast as though nothing had happened.

I have always thought of this as an example of blissful ignorance for her. At least she doesn't have to undergo the stress and fear that would surely accompany the conscious knowledge of what was happening to her.

There were also a number of 'triggers' to look out for, everyday things that might bring on a seizure. These included many of the identical triggers that can affect human sufferers of the disease, such as loud noises, flashing lights, a bump on the head, and many more.

We also discovered that overheating can be a seizure trigger and one hot day, she collapsed into a seizure after a walk and as it lasted quite some time, I called Ben for his advice. On his instructions I opened Sasha's mouth and checked her lips and gums which appeared very pale and far from their usual healthy pink. Ben explained this was due to a degree of oxygen deprivation combined with the equivalent of heatstroke and he advised me to wrap Sasha in cold wet towels to try and bring her body temperature down. This simple remedy did the trick and Sasha soon returned to normal. Thanks to Ben a potentially serious situation was avoided with nothing more complicated than a towel and cold water. Since then of course, I try to avoid taking her out in the hottest part of the day and always have a towel ready, just in case on warmer days. This has of course meant that we have to limit Sasha's 'sunbathing' time, so although she loves lying outside in the garden on warm sunny days with the other dogs, we ration her to short spells in the sunshine, for her own good.

It was also around this time that a friend of mine, fellow author and animal lover, Ed Cook from Zion, Illinois in the U.S.A. got in touch with me and told me take a look at a new group he'd formed on Facebook. When I followed the internet link he'd sent me, I found a group named *Sasha, The Wagging Tail of England.* Ed had known Sasha through various photos, videos and pieces of information I'd often posted on my own Facebook page and had decided to dedicate this new group to her in celebration of her remarkable resilience and of course, her by now rather well known wagging tail. Within one day I was amazed to see that over a hundred people had joined the group and she now has around 300 followers of her own, all interested in knowing more about Sasha, our other dogs and her life in general.

Gradually, we came to terms with Sasha's illness, knowing that it would always be there, in the background, waiting to strike out at her and we would simply have to make the most of the good times in between. Sasha was also by this time having regular three-monthly blood tests as the drugs she takes daily to help control the epilepsy, namely the Phenobarbital (epiphen), and bromide (libromide), combined with a steroid she takes for her skin allergies can lead to a build of toxins in the liver and it's essential to ensure her dosages are within acceptable levels in her bloodstream. So far all her tests have shown her to be within those parameters and we must hope they remain so.

It was with great sadness that I received a phone call one day from Ben who had called me personally to inform me he was leaving the practice to take up a new position working for a well known dog charity that has surgeries and hospitals in various parts of the country. He wanted me to hear the news from him and not by chance at a future visit to the surgery. He had become more of a friend than a vet in the time Sasha and I had known him and we would miss him greatly. And yet, even though he eventually left the practice he has remained in contact with me and is always willing to give me advice on her care and treatment; a real gentleman without a doubt.

During the next few months Sasha seemed to settle into a routine whereby the seizures would take place in a regular monthly cycle, but the clusters gradually reduced from three or four to two or three as a rule. Rebecca returned to work for a while, and once again she supervised Sasha's case but soon she had to spread her time between the practice's three surgeries in the area and more often than not, Bernard became a regular feature in Sasha's regular visits. I had known Bernard for many years as he had treated a number of our other dogs periodically, most notably Sheba, as you may recall from an earlier chapter.

Apart from her seizures and skin allergies, Sasha was and is basically an extremely healthy dog, her only other need of veterinary treatment during that period of her life being a need for treatment for a tummy bug that required medication and a couple of visits to the surgery.

The greatest fear during this short illness, which included an inability to keep her food down, was that the drugs I was administering to her through her daily tablet regime wouldn't be getting into her system
in sufficient levels to keep the epilepsy at bay. For once, fortune smiled on her and there were no complications during this particular episode.

By now of course, everyone who worked at the veterinary practice knew Sasha only too well and whenever I phoned to order more of any of Sasha's regular medication the call would invariably become elongated by whichever member of staff who replied to my request wanting an update on Sasha's latest progress, state of her health and so on. When I mentioned Sasha's webpage on Facebook, I was touched that many of the staff subscribed to it as followers of Sasha's life.

Speaking of medication, by now Sasha was taking so many tablets every day that we had to find a new way to administer them. It was impossible to give her so many tablets in her food and so I hit upon a great idea, which has worked perfectly. Juliet buys a certain High Street supermarket's own brand pork liver pâté into which I place one tablet per small mouthful of pâté. Sasha now believes that taking her medications is treat time and she comes running straight away when I shout, "Sasha, tablets!" We now refer to this delicacy as *'Sasha's Special Reserve Pâté.'*

* * *

As time passed, it began to become more and more evident that Sasha and I were growing ever closer. It soon reached a point where she would only go for walks with me. If Juliet tried to take her past the front gate on her lead, she'd simply dig her heels in and refused to move. If I came out and took hold of the lead she'd cheerfully trot off down the street with me. Talk about wilful!

Unlike most dogs, Sasha also seemed to have outgrown the usual dog toys and balls the others would spend hours chasing, fetching etc. Instead, she now decided her favourite toy was a bone! We were in the habit of buying our dogs meat-filled cooked bones from the pet shop, far safer than fresh bones as these don't splinter and therefore don't present the danger of causing digestive or other internal problems for the dogs. All the dogs love them and we'd regularly replace them when the meat content was gone and the dogs had all enjoyed gnawing on the bones for a few days. Sasha however decided that one particular bone would make an ideal toy and she would happily spend ages tossing it in the air, pushing it around the floor, leaping on it and generally having the time of her life with it. To this day, the remains of that well chewed bone have remained Sasha's very special permanent dog toy. We just don't have the heart to take it away and try to replace it with another one that she might not like as much!"

Within the home, if I left one room to go into another, Sasha would follow me. If I had to leave her at home in order to go out for whatever reason, Juliet informed me that she'd sit at the back door, looking up at it and quietly 'woofing' at the door, awaiting my return, If I go for a bath, Sasha has to accompany me upstairs where she will sit and 'guard' me by sitting or lying on the bathmat while I'm in the bath.

If I have to get up in the night for any reason which happens quite often due to the pain caused my medical condition Sasha will automatically wake up and follow me downstairs. I'll let her out in the garden and she'll happily go out and then come back into the house and wait for me to go back to bed.

Perhaps the greatest downside of her seizures is the effect they can have on our other dogs. Although most of them tend to ignore what's happening when Sasha has a seizure, a couple react in a different way, in all probability caused by their fear of what's happening to Sasha at the time. Worst affected is Digby, who we have to catch quickly when she starts fitting as he panics and will try to nip at her body if given the chance and has in the past delivered a few minor tooth marks to her by getting there before either myself or Juliet.

The worst episode of this happening occurred one day when Sasha began fitting in the middle of the day. Up until then, her fits had always taken place in the night, or in the very early morning. On this particular day, the seizure took us by surprise so much so that Digby, Muttley and even her best friend Sheba all reached her before we did. Although they appeared to be biting at her, we both noticed that they were, in their own way, trying to pull at her rather than biting her. They were attempting to make her get up!

Despite their intentions, by the time we managed to get them to leave her alone Sasha had sustained a number of small but bloody bites. A visit to the vet was required and Sasha was quickly patched up, needing nothing more than a couple of surgical staples in the worst of her wounds and a painkilling injection followed by a course of daily painkillers.

It was the only time Sasha had sustained any such injuries as a result of her epilepsy, and we couldn't really blame the other dogs who reacted merely in panic and in fairness, in their own way, as we'd observed, they were trying to help her to get up, we deduced.

This incident did however teach us another lesson in our management of Sasha's illness. From that day forward, Sasha has not been allowed to spent time unsupervised with the other dogs in the kitchen and now spends the majority of her time with me in the lounge, where I spend most of my time, on my laptop or reading etc. She loves it as she has Cassie and Penny with her for company although she spends most of the time lying next to me on the sofa, usually with her head resting on my leg, or sometimes on the corner of my laptop!

During the evening, when we allow all our dogs to join us in the lounge we ensure we keep a close eye on Sasha at all times. We're fortunate that our dogs receive sufficient exercise during the day that they all kind of 'crash out' in the evening, and all fall asleep almost as soon as they join us in the lounge. A few (we have ten dogs in total), like to stay in their beds in the kitchen so if Sasha does begin to go into a seizure, both Juliet and I are, (we hope) sufficiently well-placed to prevent any of the dogs from nipping or biting at Sasha in fear of what they simply don't understand. These are, after all, her pack mates, her canine friends, Sheba especially. We have to bear in mind that only three of the dogs, Digby, Sheba and Muttley display this particular fear reaction. The others don't seem affected by Sasha's seizures.

Sasha certainly seems to enjoy the fact that she now gets to spend most of her tie with me. The love and devotion she displays towards me goes far beyond anything I've previously experienced in my many years of owning dogs. Not only that but she seems to have developed the most incredible empathy for my own illnesses. Without going into personal details which have no place in this book, let me just say that I suffer from a number of disabling illnesses which over the years have severely affected my everyday health and my mobility. I would swear that Sasha realises this and my beautiful baby girl, always seems to sense when I'm feeling particularly down or depressed or in excessive pain, and she then becomes even more affectionate and attentive than usual as if, in her own way, she is taking care of me. She has, without a doubt, been quite inspirational for me, as, if my dog can cope with all the negatives that life has thrown at her and still be as happy and carefree as she is, who am I to complain about my own situation? More than once, I've described her to people as 'my canine angel on earth.'

Sasha also has a wonderful habit, when she walks into a room, of walking round the room, with that famous tail of hers wagging at a rate of knots as she goes from dog to dog, as though saying "Hello" to each and every one of them, before she will eventually find a place to sit or lie down, or just jump onto my lap and cuddle up and go to sleep.

In this way, we have learned to spend some wonderfully happy and joy filled days and as many loving and peaceful evenings together. Special? She most certainly is.

Chapter 12

More friends

Although this book is primarily about Sasha and her life since joining our family, it is only fair that I mention the other dogs who form her extended family within our home. I've already mentioned some of them and how they came to be with us, namely Sheba, Digby, Muffin, Petal and Penny, so here's a quick rundown on the rest of our wonderful 'pack' of rescue dogs, all of whom play their part in Sasha's daily life.

I previously mentioned Cassie in passing. Her story is quite amusing in some ways. Juliet spent some time a few years ago training to become a dog groomer and for a short time, she ran her own mobile dog grooming business, visiting client's home to clip, bathe, or carry out nail clipping or other associated grooming tasks. This small business went rather well and she gradually built up a small but loyal group of clients, until she developed carpal tunnel syndrome, and the constant pain meant she could no longer carry on the business. Nowadays she manages to groom and care for our own dogs, but even that can often cause her to be in great pain afterwards, but by only doing one or two a week, she copes admirably. This refers only to those dogs who require clipping etc, as all our dogs receive regular brushing and regular grooming, (ear cleaning, nail trimming and so one on a weekly basis).

Returning to Cassie's story, one day Juliet went as usual to carry out the grooming and clipping for one of her regular customers. Seeing the car pull up outside as she returned home, I thought I could see a small head sticking out from under her body warmer. Opening the front door, I walked out to meet her.

"What's that?" I asked, knowing exactly what 'it' was of course.

"It's a dog," she replied, with a sheepish grin on her face, doing her best to look a picture of innocence.

"I can see it's a dog, darling. What's it doing in your body warmer? Is it a stowaway?"

"She's ours."

"Since when?"

"Since now."

"How come?"

"The woman gave her to me."

"I gathered that, but why?"

"Her husband hated Cassie," she replied. "The woman can't walk much and uses a disabled scooter to get around so she can't take her for walks anymore and because they live in sheltered accommodation with a communal unfenced back garden, she can't even let her out unsupervised to go to the toilet or anything. She asked me if I'd take her and give her a good home, especially as her husband can't stand the poor dog."

"But why not?" I asked.

"Because he has to get up off his lazy backside to take her out and he can't be bothered, I think," Juliet replied as she extracted the dog from her body warmer and placed her on the lawn.

I couldn't help falling for the tiny little bundle of fur that instantly began running around in circles in the garden, her tail carried high and proud and wagging furiously. No more than twelve inches long, Cassie was a cross between a Yorkshire Terrier and an Australian Terrier, mostly grey in colour, with what appeared to be underlying golden coloured stripes. She was without doubt a very pretty little dog and although I'd given Juliet a bit of a hard time, it was really a bit of fun. No way would I turn away a little dog in need, especially one as attractive as Cassie.

At the time, she was two and half years old and is now approaching her eleventh birthday but has never slowed down. She loves going out on the playing field and running at top speed playing 'fetch' with her tennis ball or simply playing chase with the other dogs on her walk. For those who know the TV advert I'm referring to, I always refer to her as our 'Duracell dog' with never ending batteries and I joke that we've never found her 'off' switch. Nothing has ever slowed her down. People who meet her for the first time are always amazed when they discover her age, always thinking she's a puppy. To be honest, she probably has more energy than most puppies. She's cute, lovable and very, very bossy. If any of our dogs go too close to her when she'd under the coffee table in the lounge she'll literally shoot out from under the table like a Moray eel shooting out from its hiding place under the sea in search of prey. This is usually accompanied by her letting out a high-pitched screech that makes the other dog(s), even the staffies, run away and either hide or roll over on their backs with their legs in the air, definitely a case of 'small dog syndrome' and so funny to see. Not for nothing is she nicknamed 'The mad ferret.'

* * *

Have I mentioned Dexter? Couch potato Dexter? A gorgeous looking black 'Staffador', a cross between a Staffy and a Labrador, with a white chest, Dexter is now eight years old, and has been part of our family for around six and a half years. This handsome lad was unbelievably thrown from a moving car travelling at about sixty miles per hour on a motorway and was lucky to survive. A driver in a following car saw what happened and stopped to see if the dog was okay. Dexter had rolled over a few times as he'd hit the ground and somehow, he'd escaped this incredible cruelty with nothing more than severe internal bruising all over his body.

The kind and caring driver who stopped to help him took him to a vet to be checked over and Dexter ended up in a rescue centre where we first saw him. The pen in which he was held was mostly in shadow and one corner was exposed to the sun, forming a triangular sunny spot. Dexter had pulled the blanket from his bed into the sunny corner and had made himself a nice little sunbathing area. Seeing this, we assumed we'd found a really clever, intelligent dog and we had no hesitation in adding him to our family.

Only later did we discover our first impressions of Dexter's intelligence might have been slightly exaggerated.

It transpired that Dexter loved the sun alright, and would do almost anything to be out in the garden sunbathing until he was virtually cooking. Unfortunately, when it came to anything else Dexter was sadly bereft of ideas! Going for a walk had always been something of trial with our beautiful but lazy dog, as he'd rather spend the day lounging in his bed than do something as energetic as actually getting up and going out, expending his energy. On many occasions we literally have to drag him from his bed and make him go out, otherwise he'd and up as an overweight, sedentary lump. Even when he deigns to join us for a walk, he is very much of the 'stop/go' variety of dog. He will walk at his own slow pace, stopping to sniff at anything that captures his interest, probably cocks his leg up about a hundred times in the space of a thirty minute walk, mostly for the purposes of scent laying rather than actually going to the toilet, though why he bothers I don't know because if left to him, he'd never bother going down the road again. Again, I have to say he's a beautiful and loving dog, and we think that maybe his desire to spend most of his time in bed or in the garden may stem from his precious abandonment and appalling treatment in being thrown from the car. Having said that, he seems to love going for rides in the car, and when I have to take him to the vet for his inoculations or any treatment he sits in the back of the car, looking out of the windows with great interest as he watches the world go by from his vantage point. Thankfully, he shows no signs of being afraid of suffering a similar fate as he previously experienced. We all love him dearly.

* * *

Our other Staffy is Muttley who we adopted from a local dog sanctuary when he was six months old. This beautiful brindle coloured dog was part of an abandoned litter, left at the gates of the sanctuary when only a few weeks old. By the time we saw him he was one of two of the original six puppies from the litter still waiting to find a 'forever' home. The other pup was a little bitch with the same colouring and it was a difficult choice to make. In the end, we picked the boy pup because he was the most 'needy' looking of the two. The little girl appeared to be slightly more independent minded and when the lady at the sanctuary told us that not one single person had enquired about adopting Muttley in his time there, it confirmed our decision to give him a loving home.

The first few months of Muttley's life with us were a little difficult as he adjusted to living in a house rather than in a pen at the dog sanctuary. Not being used to living in a home, he systematically chewed up the kitchen skirting boards, half a dozen dog beds, the corners of various cupboard units and doors and tried to pull up the wooden parquet flooring in the kitchen, thankfully not all at once I must add. With a mixture of love, care, and patient training we were gradually able to cure him of his destructive habits and he became a calmer, home loving dog at last. Like Dexter, Muttley tends to be a 'home bod' and would happily spend his time in the house or soaking up the sunshine in the back garden. We are always amused by his habit of sitting in a large planter at the bottom of the garden that I'd filled with compost one day in preparation for adding a new shrub. He looked so happy and contented in his new 'sun lounger' that I never quite got round to planting the shrub and the planter became Muttley's favourite place in the garden on a sunny day, so much so that we nicknamed him our 'pot dog' and I even took photographs of him and showed them to friends, saying 'Look, I've grown a Staffy in a pot."

If there's a drawback in Muttley's life it's the fact that he suffers from an in-built sense of nervousness and though happy to go for a walk, he hates being let off his lead to run free. As soon as his lead is unclipped from his collar, he'll stand still beside me and will only move if I move. He's quite happy playing with his pack mates in the back garden. Where this sense of insecurity originated from we've never been able to work out, but the truth is, Muttley is happy and contended with his life, loves to cuddle up to me or Juliet in the evenings, and we wouldn't want to change him. He'll be six years old this year, so it's fair to say he's pretty much set in his ways by now.

* * *

The last of Sasha's pack mates still to be mentioned is our 'elder statesman' Dylan, the Bedlington Terrier. Dylan is another dog who was abandoned at an early age, in his case at eleven months old. Left tied to the gates of the sanctuary Dylan had clearly been beaten, whipped and very badly abused in his short life to that point. This was perfectly illustrated when we saw him for the first time and asked if we could take him for a walk to see how we got with him and vice-versa of course. As soon as the sanctuary attendant went to bring him out us and he saw the lead in her hand he literally threw himself against the back of his pen in an attempt to get away from her, a sure sign that he saw the lead as a whip or something similar and that he expected to be hit or beaten with it. We soon made the decision to adopt him, but I ended up spending the first month of his time with us sitting on the floor with him, slowly getting him to accept being touched and handled and slowly he grew to accept being gently stroked and given affection.

Eventually, he became a wonderful loving dog, and loves nothing more than running free across the fields, like Cassie very much belying his age, as he's now eleven, almost twelve years old. Sasha absolutely adores him and spends ages walking up to him wagging her tail in his face, which he often finds disconcerting and will bark at her to tell her to go away. She gets so upset to be shunned when he does that, and will always keep going back for more; she's such a glutton for punishment.

* * *

So there we are, all of Sasha's friends have had a mention now, having previously talked about the three puppies, Digby, Muffin and Petal, her best friend Sheba, and Penny, saved from the railway line. Every day is different as you can imagine and the dogs bring great pleasure to our lives, and also of course, great responsibility. None more so than the very special dog whose illness requires a greater sense of responsibility than any of the others, the beautiful Sasha of course.

Chapter 13

Emergency!

We'd settled into a pretty good routine as the months passed and Sasha's seizures, though not diminished in any way were at least taking place on a fairly predictable level. She'd go three, maybe four weeks without any seizure activity and then she'd be struck down by one, maybe two in a day, and we'd carry on having fun and enjoying ourselves in the interim periods.

Every three months, she'd go to the vet for her regular blood tests and they always showed her epiphen and bromide levels to be within the acceptable levels.

The summer had been a long and rather hot one for a change. We'd had very little rain, which was great for Sasha who hated that horrible wet stuff from the sky, and the only downside was that the heat made it difficult for Sasha to enjoy her walks as much as she usually did.

One side effect of taking the numerous medications prescribed for her was that they left her with a much improved appetite. Basically, Sasha was almost constantly hungry and would eat anything put in front of her. Because she was also taking steroids for her skin allergies, this also led to her putting on some extra weight and no matter how hard we tried to keep her weight gain down, it was impossible to totally prevent her putting on a few extra kilos.

Because of the extra weight she was carrying this made moving around in the heat of the afternoon much harder for her, and most of the time, I either took her for shorter walks in the hottest part of the day or would often wait until the cool of evening, which she still didn't like because by the time she'd had her late afternoon round of medications, she'd be feeling sleepy and wanted nothing more than to have her dinner and then crash out in the lounge.

By this time, Sasha was having to take six tablets every morning, followed by another ten in the afternoon, a lot of medication for any dog, surely, so it was no wonder she became a bit dopey. Most recently added to her medication regime was a tablet designed to give her liver support, to help prevent the build of toxins from her medications. She also had a tremendous thirst, again an effect of her medication, and could literally drain a full bowl containing six pints in one enormous drinking session, like refuelling a jumbo jet.

Most importantly of course, our baby girl was happy and living and loving life to the best of her ability, despite the ever present threat of seizures.

Summer gave way to autumn and the cooler weather was greatly appreciated by me as well as by Sasha. I hate it when it becomes too hot and welcomed the season of falling leaves and falling temperatures. Before we knew it October was consigned to history and we found ourselves in November and thoughts of Christmas began to creep into everyone's minds.

Things never seem to go according to plan though, do they? As the last week of the month approached we awoke one morning, never realising what was lurking on the horizon for my poor little Sasha.

It was mid-afternoon when she began fitting, the time being unusual in the first place. She'd only ever had one at that time of the day. I gave her the usual dose of Diazepam, she came round from the seizure and I gave her a big hug and lots of love as usual and hoped it would be just a 'one-off' incident. I couldn't have been more wrong. A couple of hours later, soon after she'd taken her medications and had devoured her meal as usual, Sasha keeled over into another seizure. Juliet and I looked at each other in surprise. This wasn't normal as far as Sasha's seizure activity was concerned. If she was going to have a second fit, it would usually closely follow the first one, maybe an hour later at most.

We could only hope that was it, end of seizures, but we were wrong, very, very wrong. As the evening wore on, Sasha appeared to have returned to normal, enjoying the usual routine of spending time on my lap, cuddled up all nice and peaceful, and heading out to the garden whenever she felt like it, but, just as we were about to settle down for the night, she went into another seizure! Now I really was becoming concerned. Poor Sasha looked worn out and even though she tried to climb the stairs to go to bed, she was too weak to make it.

I told Juliet to go to bed while I stayed downstairs with Sasha in case she suffered any further seizures. Sure enough, as I lay on the sofa with Sasha on a dog mattress on the floor beside me, she started fitting yet again, a pattern that continued all through the night, at intervals of approximately two hours.

I was more worried than I cared to admit even to myself. I'd read so many articles about dogs going into a round of seizures from which they never recovered and I had to try to stop myself from thinking that this could be happening to Sasha.

Morning dawned at long last. The night seemed to have gone on forever, and as soon as the veterinary surgery opened I phoned to tell them I was bringing Sasha in right away. By this time, she'd suffered nine seizures since they'd begun the previous afternoon. Rebecca wasn't on duty that day and Sasha was rushed in to see John, a new locum vet who I was meeting for the first time that morning. John was actually quite brilliant with her, yet another vet who was immediately enamoured with my baby girl.

She must have felt drained and really unwell but Sasha always loves meeting new people and her tail began its usual frantic wagging as soon as she met John, who advised me the best thing to do would be for them to admit Sasha as an in-patient and put her on a slow drip of diazepam and fluids to try to allow her brain activity to settle down. If all went well, Sasha might recover enough for me to collect her that night before closing time at 7 p.m.

It almost broke my heart to leave her there, knowing how ill she'd been all night and how ill she still was in reality. I knew however, that it was the best, in fact the only thing to do and so I drove home feeling tired from lack of sleep, emotionally drained and worried about Sasha in a way I'd never worried before. I lay on the sofa and tried to grab an hour's sleep but just couldn't fall asleep, so worried was I about our Baby Girl.

By lunchtime I simply couldn't contain myself and felt I had to call the surgery to ask how she was getting along. I was put through to John who told me that Sasha had suffered another seizure not long after I'd left her at the surgery that morning but had remained stable since then. He still thought it possible that I'd be able to collect her that evening and I duly arrived at the surgery at 6.30 p.m. fully expecting her to be well enough to come home with me.

The look on the receptionist's face when I walked in told me all was not well, however. She asked me to take a seat and within a minute the door to the treatment area opened and John stepped through and walked straight up to me.

"Sasha was doing fine, Mr. Porter but she went into another seizure about five minutes ago."

"Oh no," was my immediate response. I felt awful, almost speechless.

John took me by the arm and said, "Come on through to the back. You can stay with her as she comes of it. She has two nurses with her at present."

Poor Sasha was in a large crate on the floor in the centre of the treatment area, two nurses, as John had said, in attendance on her. She was still fitting, though her leg movements had slowed sufficiently to tell me she was coming to the end of what I always termed the 'active' element of the seizure. It wouldn't be truly over until she'd gone through the recovery phase and was on her feet again. My great fear by now was that with the number of seizures she'd suffered in the last twenty four hours, would she recover at all? Would her brain be damaged?

The looks on the faces of the nurses told me their fears were similar to my own. It struck me that it was possibly the first time they'd actually witnessed a dog going through a seizure from start to finish. Usually their jobs entailed taking care of a dog or cat or whatever, in the aftermath of a seizure, when the owner brought their pet in to the vet for treatment following a fit.

They would later inform me my assumption had been correct and that they were as scared as any owner would be on witnessing such a seizure for the first time. Both nurses were on the floor beside Sasha's crate, doing their best to stroke her head through the bars and the open door to the crate and talking quietly and lovingly to her, even though they must have been aware she couldn't hear them and in all probability couldn't even see them.

They made room for me to join them on the floor, a position that caused me considerable pain due to the damage to my spine, but this was Sasha, and to hell with the pain!

Having finished with his last patient, John came through to see and talk to me.

"Mr. Porter, it's really important that Sasha remains under in-patient care overnight. We don't provide the service here and she'll need to go to the emergency overnight practice. She needs constant monitoring and they can also keep her on the drip and ensure she receives immediate treatment in case of more seizures"

I knew the place he referred to which was a few miles away on the other side of town. I had to make some fast financial calculations. Although she was insured, Sasha's insurance for the current year was coming to an end and would be due for renewal quite soon but the balance of cover left on her account wouldn't be enough to cover her medications for the remainder of her insurance year and a stay at the emergency out of hours veterinary facility which I knew would be expensive.

John informed me that even if it only transpired that she needed supervision overnight without any additional medications or treatment, the cost would run into more than two, possibly well over three hundred pounds.

Worried sick, I excused myself for a few minutes, explaining I'd need to talk to my wife to try and arrange finance for her stay at the out-of-hours practice. I went outside in the fresh air to make a phone call to Juliet, and must have smoked about five cigarettes in the ten minutes I spent talking with her.

"We have to let her go there," I said to Juliet who totally agreed with me. "If we bring her home and she continues having the seizures without immediate veterinary care being on hand, we could lose her," I added.

We both knew we couldn't let that happen and we contemplated using a credit card that we only kept for dire emergencies. They didn't come much more dire than this.

Eventually, Juliet suggested she have a word with her son, Robert who lived over a hundred miles away on the coast at Scarborough. Perhaps he'd loan us the money to pay for Sasha's overnight care. I agreed and she hung up and I waited patiently for my mobile to ring, which it did within less than five minutes. Robert, a director of a large holiday complex on the east coast had agreed to finance Sasha's emergency care no matter how much it cost. His mother had always been very proud of him and his sister Rachel, both the children of her first marriage, and half-brother and sister to Rebecca and Victoria who were the children of her second unsuccessful marriage.

Her pride in her son now rose to an even greater level as she explained to me that Robert had told her he wouldn't loan us the money, he would GIVE it to us to ensure Sasha would have the best chance of pulling through. He and his sister, also a director of the company they both worked for, would share the cost between them. What a wonderful, marvellous and generous gesture!

Armed with Robert's credit card details, I re-entered the surgery and was able to inform John that the finance for Sasha's overnight care was not a problem and he immediately phoned the out-of-hours service to make the necessary arrangements. I would have to take Sasha there myself in my car as soon as she was well enough to travel.

Luckily, she now began to recover from the latest seizure and together, myself and the two nurses made such a fuss of her and they cleaned her up and placed a fresh blanket in the crate which John had said I could borrow to transport her in as he didn't want her being loose in the car in case she began fitting again, a very wise precaution.

By this time, it was already past closing time for the surgery and yet, as I looked round, not only were John and the two nurses still there, but the other on-duty nurses, and the receptionists and practice administrator were all standing at the rear of the treatment area, patiently waiting to find out how Sasha was. Every member of staff was there. They all care so much for Sasha they were giving up their own time to make sure she was okay.

John turned to them all and said, "It's past closing time, so if one of you can stay to help me lock up when Mr. Porter's gone, the rest of you can get away home."

Not one person moved. They were all so concerned for Sasha that they all stayed and waited and when Sasha had recovered enough to travel John helped me to load her into my car, still in the crate, by which time it was 7.45 p.m. and I slowly pulled away from the rear doors of the surgery, with the entire staff standing there waving us off. That was such a touching moment and proved to me, as if I hadn't already known, just how dedicated the staff at the practice are and how much they truly love my baby girl. They should have all gone home at 7 p.m. but there they were, standing in the dark watching us go and wishing us good luck.

I arrived at the out-of-hours surgery about twenty minutes later after driving across town. John had phoned ahead to let them know my estimated time of arrival and the night receptionist saw me parking my car and came out to help me. She took one look at Sasha who was peering at her as I opened the tailgate, and simply exclaimed "Oh my God, just look at that face!" Another instant conquest for Sasha.

After checking in, and giving the receptionist the credit card details to cover the fees, the duty vet came and took Sasha and me into an examination room. Luck had smiled on me and on Sasha that night as the vet was very knowledgeable on the subject of canine epilepsy. Like Ben, he'd owned an epi-dog himself. Sasha, by now, was more like herself, and showing an interest in everything in the room, her tail wagging as normal and she felt an instant rapport with the vet, giving him lots of attention which I was so pleased to see him reciprocating. If nothing else, despite my worries and fears, I could tell that Sasha was going to be in good hands for the night.

It nearly broke my heart to have to leave her again, and the look she gave me as I walked out of that room, leaving her with the vet, made me feel wretched, as though I was abandoning her.

The drive home seemed to take ages and I finally walked into the house at almost ten o'clock. I'd left home at just after 6 p.m. hoping to take my baby girl home by seven and now here I was, almost bedtime and just arriving, feeling worn out and emotionally drained. I hadn't eaten all day but just didn't feel like anything, and all I could do was sit down for a short time with Juliet as we hugged and wept for Sasha. Though neither of us actually voiced the words, I knew we were both wondering if Sasha would ever come home again or whether she'd entered into one of those terrible cycles of fits that simply couldn't be controlled, leaving her weaker and weaker until... as I said, we couldn't say it then so I'm not going to say it now.

We went to bed, we couldn't sleep. I got up, paced the floor downstairs, kept looking at the clock, then paced some more. The vet had told me that I could call at any time in the night if I just wanted to see how Sasha was, and at one a.m. I did just that. The vet informed that Sasha had gone into another fit not long after I'd left, but was now in recovery. My heart was in my mouth as I listened. It seemed that every time I left her, previously at our own vet and now at the overnight surgery, she went into a seizure soon after my departure. I couldn't help wondering if these additional fits might be associated with her becoming over-stressed each time I left her and asked the vet his opinion.

He was sure the original series of fits were purely due to some epileptic trigger but said it could be possible that a build up of 'stressers' in her brain was perpetuating the fits, and of course, being separated from me could well be taken as a major 'stresser' as she is so closely bonded to me.

While this may sound cute as a symbol of Sasha's devotion to me, at the time it served to make me feel guilty thinking that me being so close to her might have caused her to have additional fits through her feeling stressed without me. The vet did of course reassure me that such a thing was only a possibility, not a certainty.

"If you come back at around seven-thirty a.m. Mr. Porter, you can collect Sasha and then take her directly to your own veterinary surgery. They normally open at eight-fifteen so if you're a bit early, don't worry. They'll open up for you as soon as there's someone on the premises."

Thanking him I returned to the bedroom where Juliet was lying awake and filled her in with the news of the latest fit.

"Oh no," she said. "Not another one. When will it end? Poor Sasha."

"I have to take her back to our vets first thing in the morning. I need to collect her from the emergency vet at seven-thirty."

"You're not going to get much sleep," she said.

"I don't think I can sleep anyway," I replied and sure enough, neither of us slept that night, apart from short 'cat-naps' from time to time.

A quick cup of coffee was all I could manage in the morning and I was on the road again in the dark November morning. Arriving at the out-of-hours surgery I rang the bell and was ushered in by the same receptionist who'd checked us in the previous night.

"How is she?" I asked.

"She's been stable since the seizure last night," she replied. "The vet will be out to see you in a minute."

While I waited for the vet to appear, I paid the final account and soon enough he appeared and led me through to the same treatment room where we'd met the previous night.

"Before I bring Sasha in, I've been doing some additional research," he told me. "There's a drug, usually used in the treatment of human epilepsy that has only been authorised for veterinary use in extreme cases. As far as I'm concerned, Sasha's case can be classed as extreme so I feel she could benefit from the use of Keppra. You might want to talk it through with your own vet and see what he thinks."

"Yes, right, thank you," I replied, grateful to him for taking the time to seek extra helpful information that could prove useful in Sasha's treatment.

"I've made some additions regarding its use on her treatment record for your vet to consider."

By now, Sasha was growing impatient of hanging around as we talked, a sure sign she was feeling much better. After giving her a short walk round the car park so she could relieve herself, we soon had her loaded in to the crate in the back of the car, much to her disgust; she obviously wanted to assume her usual position where she could watch the world go by through the windows, but she still wasn't out of the woods and her safety was of paramount importance. Very soon, we'd be back at her own vet practice where I would find out the next steps we would have to take to make her well again. The out-of-hours vet explained that he'd left a catheter in place and also included the remaining contents of the two drips she'd been receiving through the night. He thought our own vet would want to continue their administration once she was back in their care.

Touchingly, much as had occurred at our own practice the previous night, after helping load Sasha into the crate, both the vet and his overnight receptionist/nurse stood waving as we drove out of the car park.

Sick or well, Sasha sure knows how to make an impression of people.

Chapter 14

The Third Day

The early starters at our surgery were collectively delighted to see Sasha on her feet, wagging her tail and generally looking much better than she'd been the last time they saw her the previous day. The two girls on reception as they opened the doors to admit us immediately called through to the nurses and admin staff who were in the office and treatment areas, "Sasha's back!"

Before we knew it, Sasha and I were surrounded by a host of well-wishers as the entire on-duty staff came out to see her. Sasha appeared equally pleased to see them all and her tail wagged so hard her entire rear end wagged with it, and my baby girl looked a picture of happiness. Despite the fact that I ached all over, my eyes were red and puffy from lack of sleep and worry, and my legs felt like jelly, I couldn't help but smile and for the first time in three days, I allowed myself a tiny hint of optimism.

Fortunately, John was on duty that morning and he arrived for work while Sasha's 'welcome party' was taking place.

"Be with you in a couple of minutes, Mr. Porter," he smiled as he saw Sasha bouncing with happiness. "I just need to change out of my jacket."

"Whenever you're ready, John. Sasha seems quite happy to monopolise your staff's time until you can see her," I joked with him.

He was back with me as promised a few minutes later, having changed into his veterinary uniform. Sasha and I followed John into a consulting room where we were joined by one of the practice nurses.

"Take a seat for a minute, Mr. Porter, while I quickly read through the notes from the out-of-hours practice," he said to me and I gratefully sank into the chair beside the examination table, while the nurse fussed and played with Sasha who was lapping up the attention.

"I think adding Keppra to her drug regime is a very good idea," John said after reading the notes. "I'll need to order it as it's not a normal veterinary medication and you can collect it in a few days."

He went on to explain that Keppra was what he termed a 'pulse medication,' only to be taken if Sasha suffered from multiple fits in one day. I would then need to give her the required dose for a period of just three days which was designed to reduce the excessive brain activity that can lead to seizures. After discussing the Keppra he looked at all the notes provided by the overnight vet and finally came to a decision.

"We really need to keep Sasha here again for the day, to keep her under observation. We'll continue the drips which do seem to have stabilised her condition very well over the course of the night. If she continues to improve and shows no signs of further seizure activity I see no reason why she can't go home with you this evening."

"I can hardly believe it, John. We've been so worried and thought we might be losing her."

"She's a very special dog," John replied, using the phrase so many people have used throughout Sasha's life. "She's tough, resilient and she has quite remarkable powers of recuperation."

"I can't thank you all enough. You've been wonderful with her, you really have."

"It's always a pleasure for us to see any pet recover from a serious incident like this."

"I know, John, but you and the girls have all gone a little bit further than duty demanded. I know that, for sure."

John just smiled, but thanked me for my appreciation and repeated the way we were going to approach the day. Sasha would stay with them for the day, under observation, and if she had no more fits, she could come home at tea time.

I couldn't wait to let Juliet know the potentially good news and phoned her from the car park as soon as I'd left Sasha with John, hoping that she'd now recovered sufficiently that any stress or anxiety she felt at me leaving her again wouldn't trigger any further seizures.

We were lucky, and Sasha was tough, and after a nail-biting few hours I received the phone call I'd been waiting for.

"Sasha's fine now, Mr. Porter. She's remained stable since the seizure she suffered at the out-of-hours surgery late last night. I'm satisfied the worst is over and you can collect her in a couple of hours and we can then discuss future dosages of her medications before you take her home."

I was over the moon with relief and pleasure, and sure enough, later that afternoon I arrived at the surgery to collect Sasha.

While I was waiting my turn in the waiting room, I spent some time talking to the girls on reception, both of whom told me how they all loved Sasha and they all felt they were a part of her life as she'd been coming for so long and they were so pleased she'd recovered as they'd all been afraid for her. Apparently, some of them had been in tears in the treatment room before I'd arrived two nights previously when they saw her having that awful seizure prior to my arrival. The girls actually told me they thought my wife and I were special people as well as Sasha being a special dog, because, as they put it, you had to be special to be able to see a dog going through seizures like that and have the love and the strength to go on doing so much for her and making sure she had a happy life.

I thanked them but told them we were definitely not special and that they should see the fear and worry we go through every time Sasha has one of her seizures. It's something you never get used to and even though you know they're going to occur from time to time, they always take you by surprise and cause the same feelings of helplessness and panic. It was nice of them to think like that though. I suppose not all dog owners are quite so caring?

I asked if Sasha had been fed and they laughed as they told me they'd fed her with the special food they give to dogs in recovery from operations and Sasha had totally devoured it and then looked for more. Of course, she hadn't eaten since the day she'd begun the run of seizures so she must have been ravenous. She'd certainly lost a bit of weight while she'd been so poorly. The staff at the surgery took some wonderful photographs of her after her recovery, one of which was used as the main cover photo for this book. They simply couldn't believe the sheer happiness she displayed after all she'd been through!

Soon enough, John called my name and I walked in to the treatment room to see Sasha standing waiting for me, the tail wagging (of course). After discussing Sasha's future treatment, and arranging a follow-up appointment in five days, just as a precautionary checkup when John would also do another round of blood tests to ensure everything had settled down and with the good wishes of the staff echoing in our ears, Sasha and I walked out of the surgery together. After three of the most horrendous days in the life of our baby girl, *we were going home!*

Chapter 15

Homecoming

Sasha sat up in the rear of the car, looking out through the windows as usual, the vet's crate returned to them before we departed for home. As was also quite usual, she did her 'Hound of the Baskervilles' impersonation as we drove along, howling her head off at the top of her voice which she always does as we drive along. For once, instead of telling her to be quiet, I welcomed it. That sound was like music to my ears, Sasha's own special song of joy.

She sensed she was going home and I could almost feel her excitement as we pulled up outside our house and I turned the engine off. Opening the tailgate, it was all I could do to stop her leaping out of the car onto the street.

She walked along the garden path with such happiness in her walk and Juliet was waiting just inside the tall back gate as we approached. She'd purposely kept the other dogs inside so Sasha didn't get overwhelmed the second she walked into the garden. She made such a fuss of Sasha but of course, all the other dogs knew she was there without having to see her, they could sense her presence. We gradually allowed them out to see her, one or two at a time and I can honestly say I've never seen such behaviour as they welcomed her back to the pack. They were all so happy to see her, and Sasha displayed equal joy in seeing all her doggie friends again, her tail wagging at about a hundred miles per hour, with her rear end joining in.

The next hour passed in a whirl as Sasha settled back in to her home as if she'd never been away. She strutted around the lounge, going from dog to dog, wagging her tail at them, going nose to nose in greeting, making her trade mark snuffling sounds and generally making a very definite statement that seemed to say, "I'm back!"

Once the excitement of her return had been relieved a little, Juliet took the time to look closely at her as she fussed over her and made the comment, "She's lost a lot of weight."

I hadn't realised quite how much she'd lost because I'd seen her albeit briefly each day, whereas Juliet hadn't seen her since the seizures began three days previously, so the weight loss appeared more dramatic to Juliet.

"She'll soon gain it back," I said, "and don't forget, she's overweight anyway because of the steroids."

"That's true," Juliet agreed. "Maybe we can try to keep her weight at this level?"

"I doubt it," I replied. "As soon as she gets her normal appetite back, I'm sure she'll go back to her usual weight again."

We both agreed that her weight loss, an obvious side effect of three days of near starvation would be nothing but a temporary thing and though she may look a little thinner, she was certainly not emaciated.

The first night and day following her return were fraught with worry and an unnatural sense of anticipation of the worst case scenario for us both as we watched Sasha's every movement, worried in case she suddenly relapsed into the seizures again. Once she achieved the first twenty four hours of being seizure-free and had enjoyed two short walks with me, morning and afternoon as was her normal routine, we allowed ourselves to relax a little.

Apart from being very tired and worn out from the sheer physical toll the twelve fits almost one after the other had effected on her body, Sasha was very much her normal self, and of course, we knew she at least had no recollection of the actual seizures. Within three days she seemed to have recovered completely from her ordeal and was now full of love, life and boundless energy!

That first week after her return from the brink was one in which Juliet and I were on tenterhooks twenty four hours a day as we watched and waited, and watched and waited some more, in case the seizures returned. They didn't and so with Christmas fast approaching we did our best to resurrect the Christmas spirit in time to enjoy the festivities of the holiday season.

As far as I was concerned however, I'd already received the greatest Christmas present possible. After almost losing my beautiful Sasha she was back home, as well as she possibly could be bearing in mind that the epilepsy was still there, always lurking in the background. Our hopes and our prayers and those of many others who had contacted me through her Facebook page had been answered, In particular my cousin Barbara in Birmingham spent many hours in church praying for Sasha, lighting candles for her and even had her added to the church's 'sick list' so the congregation in general were also praying for her friend, Sasha. Oh yes, she somehow forget to tell them Sasha was a dog!

Christmas drew closer and we were even more on edge as we realised that the holiday would fall approximately one month after Sasha's multiple seizure attack. Would the regular seizure pattern return? If so, there was every chance we would be faced with her suffering one or more seizures on Christmas Day or at least at some point over the holiday period.

We felt truly blessed when both Christmas and New Year passed uneventfully. Sasha and I paid a visit to the vets to deliver a very large box of chocolates and a Christmas card to the staff as our small thank you gesture to them all for their efforts through the year in helping to take care of Sasha. While we were there, one of the nurses said to me,

"Mr. Porter, we were also very afraid for Sasha. Although we see sad events every day here, if any of us had had to be part of… well, you know what I mean, it would have been the hardest thing any of us had ever had to do. We were all crying for her at various times while she was here. She's so brave and so happy and I mean it when I say she's touched the hearts of everyone who has come into contact with her here over the years."

I was so choked up by her words, knowing exactly what she meant and I almost cried myself, but Sasha seemed to sense the emotion of the moment, and wagged her tail furiously and made a big fuss of the nurse, leaving us both with big smiles on our faces.

In the final days before Christmas, we all relaxed a little and Sasha, who was doing great, and the rest of the dogs enjoyed the holiday season, receiving lots of extra dog treats and leftover turkey and tasty gravy in their dinners.

The new year began with no sign of any fits and we began to become lulled into a false sense of security as the weeks slowly added up to become the longest period we could remember without a seizure occurring. It was almost as if, as Bernard the vet told me during one of her check-ups, "She seems to have used up a whole six months-worth of seizures in one go."

Bernard had now taken over Sasha's care as John, who had been working as a locum at the practice had moved on at Christmas. Her medication regime remained unchanged and we really were finding the new fit-free Sasha a joy to behold. We began to joke that we now had 'the new, improved Sasha' and January turned into February and still, no seizures.

This false utopia for Sasha sadly came crashing down to earth on the 24th of February. At 3.40 in the afternoon, a time we didn't usually associate with her usual seizure occurrences, she collapsed in the lounge and began fitting. The seizures had returned after a massive fit-free period of *fifteen* wonderful weeks. Her seizure lasted around two minutes, about an average length of time from start to finish, followed by a recovery period of about five minutes. Of course, we expected more, but we were grateful when no follow-up seizures occurred. I phone her vet practice so they could update her records to show the latest event and received a sympathetic, "Oh no, poor Sasha, after all this time," from the duty receptionist, one of Sasha's biggest fans.

As it was only one seizure, there was no need for a visit to the surgery and life returned to normal once more. We now wondered just how long it would be before the next one occurred. Meanwhile,

Sasha just happily carried on as if nothing had happened, which of course, in her mind was quite true.

Almost a month to the day, on the 23rd March at 5 a.m. Sasha began fitting again. As with the previous month's fit this one lasted around two minutes followed by recovery time. In the past, cluster fits normally followed a fairly predictable pattern, with second and any subsequent seizures following quite closely after the first one. On this day however, just when we were thinking the early morning seizure was a single occurrence, a second fit took place at 7.15 a.m. lasting approximately the same length of time as the first one.

This time, when I phoned the vets soon after they opened that morning, I spoke to Bernard who agreed we should now use the Keppra for the first time. Sasha would receive the new medication as prescribed for a three day period, which would hopefully help to reduce any chance of further seizure activity. As no further fits took place took place in the following days, we assumed the Keppra had done its job and breathed a small sigh of collective relief.

It's almost impossible to state with certainty whether the introduction of the Keppra at that point had a long term effect of Sasha's condition, but a further six weeks would pass before she suffered another, and at present, her latest seizure, on the 5th of May. Taking place just before 7 a.m. this was a short seizure and we were pleased when no further fits took place that day.

Though she suffered from a short seizure at the end of May and two more rather longer ones towards the end of July, Sasha seems to have settled into a reasonably acceptable time lapse between fits, and it's our fervent hope that the time intervals between her seizures will remain pretty much as they are at present, although we'll settle for longer periods any time of course!

Chapter 16

A New Problem for Sasha

This chapter has been added as part of an updated second edition of Sasha's book as I felt it necessary to add the latest information on her condition for those who closely follow her life through various media.

Around the time the first edition of this story was released, I'd noticed that Sasha was exhibiting signs of difficulty when walking from time to time. She seemed to be having difficulty in putting her back legs down and was almost 'walking on tiptoes.' At first, I associated this development with the fact that her allergies had flared up during the hot summer weather, and assumed the soreness this caused in her pads and between her toes was responsible for her new mobility problem.

When it became evident that the problem was getting worse and she began having difficulty in mounting the stairs at bedtime, or even to accompany me as usual when I went upstairs for a bath, I realised it could be something more serious than a simple reaction to sore feet so made an appointment for her to see the vet, yet again.

When Rebecca examined her, she initially thought that Sasha might have developed arthritis in her lower back and my gorgeous girl was prescribed painkillers with the purpose of giving her some pain relief for a week prior to carrying out x-rays to determine the exact cause of her latest problem.

On the day of her x-rays, I dropped Sasha off at the vets, and left her for a few hours until they rang to say I could collect her. Poor baby girl was still rather groggy from the sedation when I picked her up and could only walk a couple of paces, then her legs would give way. It would take a few hours for her to fully come round from the effects of the sedatives, and we then had a nervy twenty four hour wait for the visit of her orthopaedic surgeon who would give us his opinion after studying the x-rays. As luck would have it, the surgeon was the same one who had repaired Sasha's broken leg twice when she was a puppy.

Twenty four hours passed but no phone call came. As her vet was usually so reliable, I waited until almost 7 p.m. their closing time before I phoned to see if they had news for me. As you can guess, it had been a nailbitingly long day, worry and a modicum of fear tinged with hope for good news. The receptionist explained that the orthopaedic surgeon had been operating most of the day and had only spoken to Sasha's vet, Rebecca, just before she'd had to leave for the day.

So we were left with another night of not knowing what they'd found. As is, I suppose, quite normal in such cases, we began to envisage all the worst case scenarios. Was it something so bad they wanted to delay giving us bad news? I'm sure everyone has undergone times when such irrational fears raise their heads and you begin to think the worst.

The following day, I again waited and waited for a phone call. I realised Rebecca would be conducting morning surgery so I left it until lunchtime before I called the vets yet again. They'd had so many patients that morning that Rebecca was still in surgery but I was promised she'd call me as soon as she could.

At last, soon after lunchtime, my phone rang and I saw the vet's number on my caller display. It was Rebecca at last! She apologied for the delay in getting to me, but I was just relieved to hear from her.

The news wasn't exactly bad, though equally, it wasn't especially good. On a positive note, the x-rays showed that Sasha had no skeletal damage and her bones all looked fine. The downside to this was that the orthopaedic specialist had concluded that Sasha's mobility problems stem from soft tissue damage. In other words, the ligaments in her back legs are the cause of her pain and walking difficulties.

This in itself leads us into an area of difficulty. Because of her epilepsy and other conditions, the surgeon is reluctant to perform surgery on Sasha in order to correct any ligament damage and I must say, I agree. Placing Sasha under anaesthesia for any length of time certainly isn't recommended for a dog with her conditions.

After talking it through with Rebecca, it appears as if the best way forward is to allow Sasha to undergo some physiotherapy in order to help her mobility. She will of course have to continue taking the painkillers for some time, but if they help her, that's okay with me.

Of course, the most important aspect of Sasha's health care has to be the treatment and management of her epilepsy, and though we will do everything we can to make sure she receives the best care possible for her leg problems, we must be sure that any treatment doesn't put her life at risk as any operation could possibly entail. I know our gorgeous girl will react with her usual fortitude and resilience to this latest setback as she does to every trial and tribulation. Her tail still continues its relentless wagging, she loves her daily walks and many's the time she breaks into a rn that has me clinging on to her lead for dear life as she decides to enjoy herself with a good run.

At the time of writing these final paragraphs, no further seizures have taken place and Sasha is once again living and loving her life on a day to day basis. She spends virtually all her time with me, day and night, with two walks each and every day, (except if it's raining) and loves playing with her favourite toy, that old bone she loves so much. Gravy bones remain her favourite treat though she never says no to a nice meat-filled pre-cooked bone from her favourite pet store. Oh yes, and just to add a little variety to tablet-taking time, she's discovered a new treat that helps the medicine go down…cheese triangles. She loves them!

What the future holds for our beautiful and very special 'baby girl' we cannot say. More than one vet has told us that Sasha may not enjoy the full normal average lifetime for a dog of her breed, but having come so close to losing her just a few short months ago, that is not an eventuality we care to contemplate at present.

All I can say with absolute certainty is that we have been fortunate and I repeat myself by saying blessed in having the opportunity to share in the life of one of the bravest and most resilient dogs it has been my privilege to know in many years of dog ownership.

With so many human friends and fans, in reality and through the magic of the internet, I wish she could truly understand just how much she means to so many people at home and around the world.

So, though she can't say it for herself, I guess it's up to me to say a massive THANK YOU once again to all those who care for her and follow her life and her ongoing fight against one of the most invidious and upsetting ailments that can afflict a dog. Thanks also to the many other owners of epi-dogs, past and present who I've come to know since Sasha developed the illness. Their help, support and useful information has been invaluable, so thank you Sasha for bringing new friends into my life.

Thank you also for taking the time to read her story, one that I'm pleased to say is not over, and hopefully won't be for many years to come.

To all the owners of other epi-dogs around the world I can only empathise and sympathise with the never-ending roller-coaster of emotions we go through in coping with life with our 'special' dogs and believe me, epi-dogs *are* special. They all seem to share a heightened sense of awareness and an ability to empathise with their owners and the sheer unconditional love they display towards us is a joy to behold and experience.

In all fairness, as this is her story, I believe the last word should come from Sasha, so, to everyone out there, with wildly spontaneous, happy tail wagging of course... "WOOF."

* * *

Please remember to come and see Sasha and her friends at https://www.facebook.com/groups/270003923193039/

Afterword

Since the original manuscript for the book was completed and submitted to Creativia, Sasha has suffered from one single and one cluster of three seizures. Following a full set of blood tests, and a second opinion obtained by Bernard, her general medications remain as they previously were, but in an attempt to reduce the strain on her liver it was decided to wean her off the steroids she's been taking to help with her skin allergies. Once clear of the steroids she was treated for the allergies with a new non-steroid medication, Apoquel. By using this alternative to the steroids we hoped this would reduce the strain on her liver, reducing the chances of a toxic build-up and thus helping to extend Sasha's life-span. Sadly, the Apoquel caused some nasty side-effects and was quickly replaced with an alternative drug, Atopica, plus a corticosteroid spray, which together have helped the allergies considerably without curing the problem completely unfortunately. However, if it helps Sasha, even to a small extent, it's good enough for me.

When we attended the surgery for the blood tests and check up following the change of medications, Sasha and I were ushered straight through to the main treatment area, no waiting room for Sasha. While we waited for Bernard to finish his consultation with his previous patient, Sasha was treated like a queen by the staff, and given almost free rein to explore the treatment rooms. She certainly knows her way around that place and the girls were so happy to see her and be able to interact with her on a 'well' basis, and not just when she's ill and in need of treatment. One of the staff had apparently been due to finish work prior to our appointment time but, knowing Sasha was due to come in to the surgery, she'd waited especially to see her. Another of the nurses was feeding her that special recovery food she seemed to like on her last in-patient visit, and Sasha was loving gently licking the food from her hand.

When Bernard was free he came in to the treatment room and carried out her examination there rather than going into a consulting room. Sasha certainly got the 'royal' treatment. Unlike some dogs who tremble and show fear on having to visit the vet, Sasha seemed to treat the entire time we were there like one big 'Sasha party' and that's a testament to the wonderful care and devotion the staff show her at every opportunity. One of them even told me I should bring her in every week, "just to say hello."

I'm sure Sasha and the staff would love it, though I'm not sure the vets themselves would appreciate such regular disruption to the working day.

What a nice thought though!

About the Author

Brian L Porter is an award-winning author, whose books have also regularly topped the Amazon Best Selling charts. Writing as Brian, he has won a Best Author Award, and his thrillers have picked up Best Thriller and Best Mystery Awards. His short story collection *After Armageddon* recently achieved Amazon Bestseller status and his moving collection of remembrance poetry, *Lest We Forget*, is also an Amazon best seller

Writing as Harry Porter his children's books have achieved three bestselling rankings on Amazon in the USA and UK.

In addition, his third incarnation as romantic poet Juan Pablo Jalisco has brought international recognition with his collected works, *Of Aztecs and Conquistadors* topping the bestselling charts in the USA, UK and Canada.

Brian lives with his wife, children and of course, Sasha and the rest of his wonderful pack of ten rescued dogs.

He is also the in-house screenwriter for ThunderBall Films, (L.A.), for whom he is also a co-producer on a number of their current movie projects.

A Mersey Killing and the following books in his Mersey Mystery series have already been optioned for adaptation as a TV series, in addition to his other novels, all of which have been signed by ThunderBall Films in a movie franchise deal.

Other Books by the Author

Thrillers by Brian L Porter

- A Study in Red - The Secret Journal of Jack the Ripper
- Legacy of the Ripper
- Requiem for the Ripper
- Pestilence
- Purple Death
- Behind Closed Doors
- Avenue of the Dead
- The Nemesis Cell
- Kiss of Life
- **The Mersey Mystery Series**
- A Mersey Killing
- All Saints, Murder on the Mersey
- A Mersey Maiden
- (Coming soon) – A Mersey Mariner
- (Coming soon) – A Very Mersey Murder

- (Coming soon) – Last Train to Lime Street
- (Coming soon) – A Mersey Ferry Tale

Short Story Collections

- After Armageddon (Amazon bestseller)
- (Coming soon) – A Meeting of Minds, co-author, Carole Gill

Remembrance Poetry

- Lest We Forget (Amazon bestseller)

Children's books as Harry Porter

- Wolf (Amazon bestseller)
- Alistair the Alligator, (Illustrated by Sharon Lewis) (Amazon bestseller)
- Charlie the Caterpillar (Illustrated by Bonnie Pelton) (Amazon bestseller)

Coming soon

- Tilly's Tale
- Dylan's Tale
- Hazel the Honeybee, Saving the World, (Illustrated by Bonnie Pelton)
- Percy the Pigeon, (Illustrated by Sharon Lewis)

As Juan Pablo Jalisco

- Of Aztecs and Conquistadors (Amazon bestseller)

Printed in Great Britain
by Amazon

33328621R00071